WEDDING FLOWERS

WEDDING FLOWERS

More than sixty beautiful arrangements
for a very special day

FIONA BARNETT

Photographs by DEBBIE PATTERSON

Text by Mary Trewby

conran
OCTOPUS

First published in 1991 by
Conran Octopus Limited
2-4 Heron Quays
London E14 4JP
www.conran-octopus.co.uk

Reprinted 1993, 1995, 1999

This paperback edition
published in 1995 by
Conran Octopus Limited

British Library Cataloguing in Publication Data
Barnett, Fiona
Wedding flowers: more than 60 beautiful arrangements
for a very special day
1. Weddings
I. Title
745.926

ISBN 1 85029 685 5

Art Director   Mary Evans
Editor   Denise Bates
Designer   Louise Bruce
Production   Julia Golding
Illustrations   Vanessa Luff
David Downton

Typeset by Litho Link Limited, Welshpool, Powys, Wales
Printed in Hong Kong

CONTENTS

INTRODUCTION

Whether grand or intimate, wildly extravagant or on a shoestring budget, most weddings feature flowers and they are surely one of the most wonderful ways of bringing colour, life and individuality to any ceremony. Yet flowers are definitely one of the trickier areas on the whole wedding agenda, often because someone involved feels they ought to be able to handle the whole thing themselves, either as a way of saving money or because they don't want to waste all those evenings spent on flower-arranging courses. Often, however, as the day draws nigh, the enthusiastic volunteer begins to realize that decorating a marquee and a church and producing forty table arrangements, as well as bouquets for the bride and bridesmaids – and all to a standard which is not going to mean that they can never show their face at the flower-arranging class for the rest of the decade – is not as straightforward as they imagined. Having said that, however, with enough planning and a little skill all that enthusiasm can be usefully harnessed and the whole experience of creating the flowers for a wedding can be an extremely fulfilling and satisfying one.

Even if you have no intention of touching the flowers, let alone attempting to arrange them, I hope very much that this book will help you. In my experience, the stipulations of many brides are very simple – 'No carnations, no chrysanthemums, no fern, and I don't want it to look like this (producing photograph) under any circumstances'. That's fine, but it reduces the options by just about one percent. A more constructive approach, perhaps, is to look at a variety of examples, taking something from here, an idea from there, until you have built up the individual result that is right for you. Inspiration can come from so many sources – a stunning combination of colours which you notice on a country walk, an architectural style you particularly admire. The possibilities are endless, as you will see from the very varied themes featured in this book, and with a little help a good florist should be able to interpret your ideas.

Above all, I hope that this book will offer inspiration and, in showing that the most unexpected materials can produce the most breathtaking results, encouragement to indulge your wildest floral fantasies. Don't be afraid to give full rein to your imagination – nothing is too huge, too tiny, too bizarre or too expensive if it's what you really want!

Fiona Barnett

SPRING

Nature's cycle begins anew and the
earth wakes up from its winter
dormancy to try on bright new spring
colours. Traditionally the perfect time
for marriage with its symbolism of
rebirth and new beginnings, spring
has a feeling of freshness and
anticipation in the air, accentuated by
the astonishing rates of growth of
flowers and foliage, which seem to
force their way out of the earth
overnight.

PERFUME IN SPRINGTIME

BRIDE'S BOUQUET
(left)
*The heady aroma of this
cascading shower bouquet will
fill any church or house with
the delicious scents of the
season.*

SPRING SCENTS
(left)
*Butterfly-like sweet peas,
particularly the old-fashioned
variety, have a heavenly
perfume; in France, the lily-of-
the-valley is traditionally given
at the height of springtime, on
May Day.*

The sensuous fragrances of spring perfume the air and lighten the heart. The first bulbs are sprouting, trees are festooned with blossom, birds are singing and the garden is illuminated with lovely patches of colour and all the subtle tonal variations of green. Great bowls of freshly cut flowers can fill a house with scent, bringing the garden indoors, and guests will be enchanted by a bride who carries wonderful perfumed blooms, releasing spring fragrances as she walks.

All the flowers chosen for this wedding have a wonderful scent. The only exception is the ranunculus, which compensates for its lack of smell with a lovely appearance. Looking like flaky pastry or crinolines with layers and layers of petticoats, ranunculus is also very long-lasting. In any case, the scented sweet peas, perfumed leaves of *Genista* (cultivated broom), fragrant clusters of lilac and slightly spicy lily-of-the-valley are a heady enough mixture. Hyacinths and unusual sweet-smelling tulips add to the perfumed potion.

The muted beauty of crisp whites and deep rich creams underplays the glorious perfume that fills the air. In fact, these are the colours of many of the scented plants of spring. Accompanied only by the green of the leaves, the flowers produce chiaroscuro patterns of light and shade that make much of the texture and forms of the materials. The restricted palette draws attention not only to the fragrance but also to the exquisite shapes of the flowers and foliage. By combining large flowers with small ones, simple blooms with clusters and flat sweet peas with bell shapes, subtle, visually interesting arrangements have been created.

BRIDE'S BOUQUET

The petals of the white 'Aladdin' tulip are pointed, and the ends curl out so that when the flower opens it is like a star and reveals a blue-ish centre. This wonderful bloom is the focal flower of the brides's shower bouquet (see page 136). All the flowers included are wired but left on the stem. Clouds of white lilac, masses of crumbly cream and white sweet peas, the daisy-like marguerites, and tendrils of lily-of-the-valley are magnificent companions. The arrangement is built up carefully to create an interesting profile (see page 133) which is achieved by varying the lengths of the stems. The handle is taped and ribboned, then completed with a bow: like the inside of a couturier dress, the back of a bouquet should look as beautifully finished as the front.

PALETTE OF FLOWERS

Lily-of-the-valley
Sweet pea
Lilac
Hyacinth
Tulip
Ranunculus
Genista (cultivated broom)
Marguerite

Pittosporum foliage

BRIDESMAID'S BASKET

A light wickerware trug-shaped basket is carried by the bridesmaid. Filled with a dazzling display of whites and creams, the basket is lined with plastic then a block of florist's plastic foam is wired in. Pittosporum, with its dark brown twiggy stem, tiny green leaf and natural curving lines, provides a solid yet delicate-looking base for the white ranunculus, lilac, the cream and white sweet peas and the lilies-of-the-valley, the latter wired into little bunches. Despite its charmingly loose look, the placing of the flowers is tightly controlled: the different coloured sweet peas are set on opposing diagonals, the lilac is recessed (see page 133), and the main flower, the ranunculus, is evenly scattered throughout. The flowers trail over the sides of the trug and sweep to a graceful point at each end, while the bouquet's profile (see page 133) is softly domed. A soft green taffeta ribbon is wound around the handle (see page 140) and ends in a long sweeping bow at each side.

BRIDESMAID'S BASKET
(above)
The luxuriant creams and lush green shades of the season and its flowers are echoed in the creamy fabrics worn by the bride and bridesmaid.

BRIDE'S BOUQUET
(far left)
The opulent effect of the bouquet is achieved by recessing blooms deep within the arrangement, giving it depth and substance.

BRIDESMAID'S BASKET
(right)
The dense, tumbling design of the bouquet is continued in the bridesmaid's basket arrangement, which cascades over the edge of a wickerware trug. The main flower is the ranunculus, which in spite of its delicate-looking layers of petals is actually very long-lasting. Lilac and cream and white sweet peas provide a delicious scent.

TABLE ARRANGEMENT
(right)
This composition for a small table is given a more rounded, compact shape; the 'Aladdin' tulips, which as the main flowers are distributed throughout, seem to stretch out their pointed petals from amidst the mass of other blooms. For an arrangement with a totally different shape and style, the 'Aladdin' tulips would work well left full length, used in a tall container with other long-stemmed flowers.

TABLE ARRANGEMENT

The white 'Aladdin' tulips used so successfully in the bride's bouquet are the focal point of the table arrangement. It, too, is made in a trug-shaped basket but, instead of being oval, the arrangement is round. An outline is created with pittosporum, white lilac and *Genista*, a cultivated broom which has creamy pea-shaped flowers, making a beautiful background for the tulips, cream hyacinths, white and cream sweet peas and bunches of lily-of-the-valley. In a taller vase, the tulips could be left full length, and used with long pieces of broom and lilac and long-stemmed sweet peas.

The bride may prefer to carry a smaller posy, perhaps incorporating lily-of-the-valley and lilac. Alternatively, freesias, with their funnel-shaped flowers and distinctive spring fragrance, come in all shades of white and cream and look wonderful in a bouquet or table arrangement. There are a number of sweet-smelling narcissii, such as the small creamy yellow 'White Sail', that could be included, along with sprigs of jasmine, the waxy pinkish-white flowers of *Viburnum × burkwoodii* which are borne in clusters, and woody branches of creamy yellow honeysuckle.

Spring produces a glorious array of fragrant white and cream blooms, and by mixing different forms – for example, the statuesque tulips, lacy lilacs, dainty lilies-of-the-valley and delicate sweet peas used here – it is possible to create subtle compositions and beautiful medleys of scents.

CLOUDS OF BLOSSOM

BRIDE'S BASKET
(left)
*The classic shades of cherry
and apple blossom are
enhanced by a vibrant blue
ribbon.*

LYCH-GATE DECORATION
(left)
*The first taste of the glories that
are to come greet guests before
they even enter the church,
with this spectacular arch of
blossom.*

Glorious displays of branches laden with blossom overhanging a light carpet of fallen petals are one of the most charming signatures of springtime. A glimpse of an orchard full of trees weighed down with blossom provokes the deepest feelings of well-being. The lovely mass of tiny flowers which covers trees that have been bare for months marks the beginning of nature's cycle of reproduction, bringing promises of plenty in the months ahead and signalling a time of hope.

For a spring wedding, clouds of white and the palest pink blossom make a ravishing arrangement. The froth of flowers has a papery delicacy which is in deep contrast to the sturdy, often gnarled branches. Using blossom decoratively is a simple approach, and even when the petals start to fall the arrangements still look striking. The wonderful shapes of the branches have an immediate visual appeal and, in these arrangements, their sculptural qualities are underlined by the addition of long branches of whitebeam with its nutty brown stem, an ovate-shaped sage green leaf with a silvery underside, and clusters of little white buds.

BRIDE'S BASKET

The bride carries a trug-shaped basket filled with branches of blossom. The basket is lined with plastic and a piece of florist's plastic foam is wired in (see page 140), then branches of cherry blossom and apple blossom and white-beam are arranged to make a soft oval shape which tapers to a long point at each end. A deep blue silk ribbon wrapped over the handle and tied in a loose, generous bow adds a streak of glorious colour to finish the bouquet.

Blossom on its own can be difficult to arrange as a bouquet because it has a tendency to look rather jumbled. However, it works well when the perimeters are well defined, as in the bride's basket. The opposite approach is to use blossom on a massive scale, exploiting its natural length – for instance, in a huge, tied bunch designed to be carried over the arm or in an enormous bouquet that almost sweeps the floor, like the lovely arrangement in Woodland Romance (see page 72), where much is made of the natural shape of the materials. Unstructured, medium-sized shower bouquets are the least successful.

LYCH-GATE DECORATION
(left)
*The porch of a church or house
could be decorated with swags
of blossom or greenery in a
similar manner to this
lych gate.*

PEDESTAL ARRANGEMENT
(right)
*The inexpensiveness of
blossom means it can be used
with abandon for
lavish arrangements on a
grand scale.*

PALETTE OF FLOWERS

Apple blossom
Cherry blossom

Whitebeam

LYCH-GATE DECORATION

Great branches of pink cherry and white apple blossom decorate the lych gate of a charming old country church. Starting from the central pair of columns, branches are tied on with gardening twine, then other pieces of blossom are pushed in to create a feeling of depth and fullness. A large quantity of blossom has been used here, although the decoration could be confined to the front of the lych gate. As a finishing touch, a swag of blossom is tied on to each gate and secured with dusty pink and blue grosgrain ribbons.

Cherry and apple blossom are widely available in flower markets in season. However, a huge mass of other plants that grow in abundance – for instance, cow parsley, early-flowering umbellifers that have been allowed to run rampant, or branches of elder with its clusters of tiny star-shaped flowers – can be used to decorate the lych gate, or a church or house porch, in the same way.

PEDESTAL ARRANGEMENT

A traditional Oriental combination of blossom and blue-and-white porcelain is the inspiration for the pedestal arrangement. However, rather than taking a stylized approach and using just one or two sculptural branches, as in Oriental arrangements, a great mass of cherry blossom celebrates the cheerful promise of spring. Secured in chicken wire (see page 133), the laden branches are complemented by the silvery white beauty of whitebeam. This lovely, full effect is one that is satisfyingly easy to achieve.

Similar, but even larger arrangements also look wonderful. Containers can range from huge terracotta pots to plain galvanized buckets or milk churns, with the height and width of the blossom full and overflowing, balancing the composition. At the other end of the scale, individual flowers could be picked from the branches, wired and used to create a garland headdress or to decorate a comb, dress or shoes.

COLOUR AND ELEGANCE

One flower accompanied only by its own leaf and thin strands of grass must have great distinction if it is to stand alone. The tulip combines an undeniable elegance with a lyrical beauty and splendid nobility. Its clear, unfussy lines make it a perfect choice for a small city wedding where strong forms and minimal colours are more appropriate than delicate blooms, lavish bouquets and harmonious colours. Using one flower in three sharply contrasting colours is stylish and assured – setting deep purple against bright orange may seem daring, but it is wholly successful.

Native to the Middle East, tulips were introduced into Europe from Turkey in the sixteenth century. The Dutch became passionate about them, exporting the bulbs to neighbouring countries and to North America and, like the exotic fruits such as the pineapple, the tulip soon became a very desirable symbol of wealth. There are fifteen recognized species or cultivated forms of tulip, all with goblet-shaped flowers of six petals.

These are flowers that have a solitary splendour and can stand on their own, without additional foliage and transitional material. The bride who chooses such blooms may well be dressed in a sleek suit rather than a voluminous gown and veil and the simple combination of deep purple and rich cream tulips sets her apart in the chicest way possible. To differentiate the bride's flowers further, the petals of her corsage and bouquet have been turned out so that the flowers have an open shape rather than the characteristic goblet of the tulip.

BRIDE'S BOUQUET

The simplicity of line in the bride's wired shower bouquet belies the skill required in making it: there is no room for covering up mistakes in a bouquet such as this. The flowers are wired individually and positioned according to size. The largest flowers form the focal point from which the other blooms and leaves are bound, with the top third made up of smaller tulips, which are angled to curve back over the wrist and make a charming crescent shape. The tulip stems are cut to length – between 5-10 cm (2-4 in) – and wired. Arranging the cream and purple tulips according to size and varying the angles at which they are wired into the binding point creates an elegant-shaped bouquet which is visually balanced and has an interesting profile. Arum lilies, the great trumpet-shaped cream flowers, could be used in a similar way to dramatic effect.

BRIDE'S CORSAGE
(right)
The unusual effect of these silken, almost black, tulips is achieved by turning back the petals. The tulip originated in Turkey and it is easy to understand the great excitement, almost a mania, in fact, which the importation of this extraordinary flower into western Europe – and later North America – sparked off.

GROOM'S BUTTONHOLE
(right)
A single, exotically striped parrot tulip is edged with the petals of an orange 'Aladdin' tulip in this highly individual buttonhole. The colour range of tulips is probably greater than that of any other flower – every year many new varieties and colours are introduced. With such an abundance it should not be difficult to find striking colours which fit in with the scheme of your wedding.

BRIDE'S CORSAGE

The bride's corsage of purple tulips curves over the shoulder in the style favoured by 1940s movie stars. Five perfect flowers, rich and velvety, are wired individually and positioned according to size (see page 139). The binding point is behind the largest flower, which is placed about a third of the way down the corsage and sits on the front of the shoulder. Because the blooms are wired individually they can be carefully controlled and moulded – the small top flower here has been designed to bend over the shoulder.

GROOM'S BUTTONHOLE

A second colour, orange, is introduced in the groom's buttonhole. It is a flamboyant choice, startling in its unexpectedness. The frilly-edged orange parrot tulip opens like a rose and is edged with petals of the fragrant orange 'Aladdin' tulip, which have been stitched then taped to the double-leg mounted parrot tulip's stem (see page 134). Bear grass is used to add a three-dimensional finishing touch; three strands of different lengths are mounted together on silver wire, taped, then looped around the flowerhead.

PALETTE OF FLOWERS

'Aladdin' tulip
Parrot tulip

Bear grass

TABLE ARRANGEMENT

Long thin bear grass adds a sharp, linear dimension to the cream, purple and orange tulips brought together for the table arrangement. So that nothing distracts from the drama of the flowers, a silver ice bucket is used as a container. The striking combination of purple and orange is one seldom used in flower arranging, but the two colours are, in fact, opposite each other in the colour spectrum and have a natural affinity as contrasting partners. The cream tulips provide visual respite from the bright orange and the deep, almost black, purple, and hence balance the arrangement.

To complement the carefully constructed bouquet, corsage and buttonhole, the arrangement has a simplicity and lovely free-flowing effect. The ice bucket is filled with chicken wire and water, the bear grass – several strands together – is used to create an outline, and the different coloured flowers are distributed evenly throughout in a generous dome shape (see page 142). The strength of these sharply contrasting colours used together is undiminished by the loose arrangement; instead, the fine lines of the grass subtly point up the linear qualities of the flowers.

TABLE ARRANGEMENT
(left and below)

EASTER WEDDING

The drifts of bluebells blooming on banks and fields during spring are a lyrical counterpoint to the golden-yellow daffodils that often accompany them. Blue and white are the colours of the most ephemeral of earthly things: the deep blue sea with the froth of white waves, the clear blue sky with puffs of cottonwool clouds floating across it. Synthesized by the Chinese in their beautiful porcelain, the combination of blue and white is reinterpreted in these lovely flowers for an Easter wedding.

Too often, it is easier to choose the obvious. Time and again, at Easter time, the colours of wedding flowers are restricted to yellow and white. Blue and white is perhaps a more unusual choice, but just as seasonal. It allows infinite variations and is a stronger combination with an extraordinarily varied palette, ranging from the pure paint-box blues of delphinium and cornflowers, through to the paler pink-tinged blues of bluebells and scabious, to the blue-violets and deep purples of irises and gentians. Whites sharpen the impact of the blue, giving it vitality and delicacy. Adding rich creams softens the compositions, introducing welcome touches of warmth.

BRIDE'S POSY

Fern and Solomon's seal make a natural edge to the bride's hand-tied posy (see page 136). There is a pleasant harmony in the juxtaposition of fine feathery ferns with the palmate shape of delphinium leaves, of the floppy white sweet peas with the lacy umbels of cow parsley, of the showy delphinium bells with the little soft blue-violet bluebells.

Like spring itself, the blooms in the bouquet exhibit a graceful exuberance. Because the material is used on its natural stems, the flowers nod their heads as they do in the fields. The ferns are wired together in little groups and spiralled (see page 136), with the bluebells, sweet peas, delphiniums and cow parsley. Because their soft stems would be cut by the binding twine, the bluebells are protected by the ferns and Solomon's seal used on the outer edge.

BRIDE'S POSY
*The flowers and porcelain
show a natural affinity.*

PALETTE OF FLOWERS

Bluebell
Sweet pea
Delphinium
Lilac
Passion flower
Cow parsley
Solomon's seal

Fern
Delphinium leaves
Passion flower trails

BRIDESMAID'S HEADDRESS

The headdress for the tiny bridesmaid is based on a potted passion flower plant grown on a wire hoop. In this instance the wire is left on when the plant is removed from the pot and joined at the back. This is a very simple way to make a charming headdress which sits beautifully on the head (if the plant is grown on a cane it is easy to weave through the trails and join them together). One passion flower has opened fully, and the extraordinary saucer-shaped bloom with its spectacular corona of purple and white filaments is complemented by bluebells and pale blue delphinium heads. These are wired into little bunches and secured on the front half of the headdress (see page 138), creating a tiara-like effect. In this instance, the foliage of one passion flower is sufficient; individual leaves may be wired on if necessary or if a fuller headdress is desired. The same materials can be broken down, wired and used to create a garland headdress. However, this structured look is more time-consuming and complicated to create, and, in any case, it would seem a pity not to take advantage of the passion flower plant's natural trails.

BRIDESMAID'S HEADDRESS
(right)
The most striking element of this headdress, the exquisite passion flower, is a bloom naturally associated with Easter as it is said to symbolize aspects of the Crucifixion.

EASTER PALETTE
(below)
Eggs could be painted in traditional Easter fashion and incorporated in the wedding arrangements.

BUTTONHOLES
(above)
on an antique egg rack

TABLE ARRANGEMENT
(right)
with a basket of tiny eggs

BUTTONHOLES

The charming trio of buttonholes might also double as corsages. The first is a small posy of wired sweet peas, bluebells and cow parsley, finished with leaves of Solomon's seal. A second buttonhole is created from two little pieces of white lilac left on their stems, crossed and bound together with wires (see page 134). The wires are then tapered and used to pin on the buttonhole behind the lapel, while the stems are displayed in front. Five delphinium flowerheads are wired individually and combined with leaves of Solomon's seal to make the third buttonhole.

On the same blue-and-white theme, the possibilities available for springtime weddings include a simple Alice band with bluebells and cow parsley attached, or perhaps three open passion flowers wired to a comb. A long flowing bouquet featuring the sweet peas and other flowers used here should omit the bluebells, which are difficult to wire because of their soft stems, or a shower bouquet with longer fronds of fern and trails of Solomon's seal would work well.

TABLE ARRANGEMENT

In the centre of a small round table, a mossy terracotta plant pot holds a composition of bluebells, pendulums of white lilac, Solomon's seal and cow parsley. The pot is lined with plastic and filled with florist's plastic foam. Full advantage is taken of the wonderful natural line of the long-stemmed Solomon's seal to make the outline shape of the arrangement. If the stems of the bluebells are not strong enough to push into the foam, they should be mounted on wire (see page 134). The arrangement is very simple, its success relying on a balanced distribution of the flowers, and skilful use of the materials.

ART NOUVEAU

BRIDE'S BRACELET
(left)
*The Art Nouveau theme is
particularly suitable for an
intimate, sophisticated
wedding and sleek satin and
creamy lace are the perfect
fabrics to accompany the
supremely elegant flowers.*

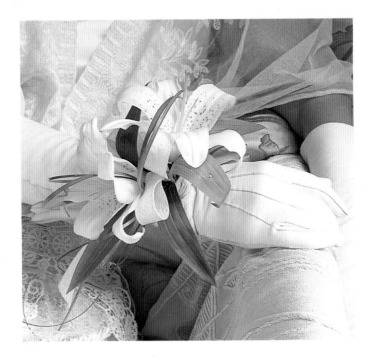

BRIDE'S BRACELET
(left)
*This strikingly individual
design is constructed like a
corsage. The carefully
positioned leaves frame the
flowers and reinforce the star
shape of the lilies.*

The arum lily is an elegant symbol of Art Nouveau, the turn-of-the-century art movement that challenged the values of the new machine age and, at the same time, was a reaction against the studied naturalism of the Impressionists. The flower embodies all the sculptural and linear qualities the artists saw in Celtic and Japanese art, which were among the eclectic influences which inspired the movement, with their emphasis on decorative line and two-dimensional, almost abstracted, pattern. The lily's generous curved and twisting shape was regarded as almost a stylized version of nature itself.

BRIDE'S BRACELET

An elegant alternative to the bouquet, a bracelet made of white 'Star-gazer' lilies – star-shaped and speckled with pink – is perfect for a small wedding, or the bride may choose to carry the bouquet during the wedding ceremony and wear the bracelet at the reception.

One of the three lilies is a bud and about 5 cm (2 in) of stem has been left on it; the others – a full bloom and a half-opened flower – have 2.5 cm (1 in) stems. The bracelet is made in the same way as a corsage, with the individually wired flowers positioned according to size, from the bud at the longest point to the fully opened one at the top with the binding point directly behind it (see page 139). Lily leaves are fanned out around the back and sides of the flowers, and two are recessed (see page 133) in order to give the bracelet a feeling of depth. As in the bouquet, three strands of bear grass, wired together at each end, are looped around the top of the open flowers, creating a graceful, linear effect and emphasizing the sinuous curves of the lilies.

Two white satin bows are inserted underneath the main flower, so that when you look into the bracelet the fabric and the bows are visible. To finish the bracelet, the wired stems are divided into two parts and taped separately, then covered in ribbons. The bracelet is bent around the wrist and tied with a bow. When the wires are pulled apart, the flowers and foliage will shift but, because all the materials are wired and are positioned correctly, they can be manoeuvred back into place on the wrist.

BRIDE'S BOUQUET

The stately elegance of the arum lily is exhibited in the bride's bouquet. A very formal wired shower (see page 136), the simple lines and minimal materials of the bouquet belie the degree of skill required to execute it well. The glorious trumpet-shaped lilies, with their creamy-white petals the texture of handmade paper and powdery yellow spadix, are accompanied only by *Fatsia japonica* and aspidistra leaves and fine threads of bear grass.

The sculptural qualities of the materials – the large, palmate *Fatsia* leaves, the broad, lance-like aspidistra and the cone of the arum lily – are underscored by the restricted, but very rich, palette of deep glossy greens and the light lime green that edges the solitary lily petal. Trails and loops of bear grass are used to soften the composition. The bouquet is beautifully balanced with a very sinuous profile.

Stems of five arum lilies, which are graded according to how open the blooms are and the size of the heads, are cut to length. Wiring must be done carefully because the stems are fairly hollow and tend to snap easily: two heavy gauge wires are pushed up the stem, which is then mounted on another wire and taped to keep in the moisture (see page 134). The aspidistra and *Fatsia japonica* leaves are very strong and stitching is not necessary, although their stems need to be wired. The leaves have been cleaned with cotton wool soaked in milk, which brings out their glossiness (proprietary leaf cleaners leave them quite sticky).

The bouquet's binding point is behind the largest lily, and the remaining flowers are wired around that, with the two longest sweeping downwards and the shorter stemmed blooms positioned to the side and above the focal flower (see page 133). The three *Fatsia* leaves are concentrated around the focal flower; the three aspidistra leaves are positioned throughout the bouquet, and the bear grass, strands of which are wired together in bunches, is left to trail freely or looped over the focal flower.

TABLE ARRANGEMENT

In contrast to the detailed work of the bouquet and bracelet, the table arrangement is very simple. Arum lilies, aspidistra leaves and arum lily stems which have been cut on an angle are arranged in a tall glass vase. Chicken wire is obviously inappropriate in a clear container, so cellophane has been scrunched up and placed in the bottom of the vase to lift up and support the arrangement – when the vase is filled with water, the effect is like crushed ice.

PALETTE OF FLOWERS

Arum lily
'Star-gazer' lily

Fatsia japonica
Aspidistra
Bear grass
Lily foliage

BRIDE'S BOUQUET
(left)
AND TABLE ARRANGEMENT
(below)
With their simplicity of line and form, arum lilies are surely the quintessential Art Nouveau flowers. Sculptural blooms such as white anthuriums or bearded irises would also be suitable.

SUMMER

The glorious sunshine of long
summer days coaxes plants and
flowers in every nook and cranny of
the garden into voluptuous displays
of colour and scent. The combination
of heady perfumes, exuberant hues
and the sheer abundance of summer
blooms makes this truly a season of
the senses.

COTTAGE GARDEN

*A*ll the romance of the old-fashioned cottage garden – a lovely tangled mass of blooms, glorious colours and fragrant perfumes – is captured for this midsummer wedding. You can almost hear the hum of bees and insects, enjoy the sweet-smelling timeless charm, and revel in the beautiful, graduated tones of red and blue and the cool creams and whites among a tapestry of greens. One of the most charming qualities of the cottage garden is its delightful air of cheerful informality, as a riotous mass of flowers of different colours, heights, shapes and sizes jostle and tumble over one another, and such a theme and setting would be suitable for any relaxed summer wedding, large or small.

Old-fashioned flowers from lovely herbaceous borders have such strong associations with summer. At no other time of the year are the colours so extraordinarily clear, the shapes so varied, the blooms so bountiful or the perfumes so strong. The heat of the day seems to intensify all the glories of the garden and sharpen the senses. It is the perfect time for love and marriage.

BRIDE'S HAIR DECORATION
(right)
A thick band of intensely coloured blooms crowns the bride's head. It is created from flowerheads and clusters of flowers wired on to a wide velvet band.

BRIDE'S BOUQUET
(right)
The blue garden trug carried by the bride is charmingly appropriate to a cottage garden theme, as if she had just stepped out into the garden that morning to gather up her blooms. When it is not being carried, the trug is temporarily eclipsed by the exuberant flowers spilling over the sides.

HAIR DECORATION

The bride wears typical blooms of midsummer in her hair. The flowers, which are wired on to a wide velvet-covered Alice band and built up into a thick mass, look as if they have just been picked from the cottage garden. Aquilegia, the delicate-looking, funnel-shaped flower also known as columbine, is cream with a yellow centre and pink edges; it has a very fine but strong stem and each flower is double-leg mounted on short silver stub wires then taped (see page 134). White saponaria is wired into very small bunches. Flowerheads of deep pink sweet william are picked from the main head and wired together. Stripy pink godetia and blue and pink delphinium flowers are taken off the main stem and wired individually on 4 cm (1½ in) stems then taped (see page 134). Clusters of the tiny star-shaped flowers of the *Alchemilla mollis* plant, which also has the delightful name of 'Lady's mantle', are wired into bunches, as is euphorbia, a very cottagey plant with florets of tiny flowers.

BRIDE'S BOUQUET

A glorious tied bouquet overflowing from a pale blue painted trug contains the same luscious colours that the bride wears in her hair. Pink peonies, the densely packed stems of blue, purple and red delphiniums, and purple michaelmas daisies with yellow centres are used with white saponaria and pink sweet william. The wonderful lime green foliage of Jacob's ladder, lacy clusters of cow parsley and the delicate white meadowsweet are allowed to trail over the edges. The stems of these typical country flowers are spiralled to make a fairly long flowing bunch (see page 136), then laid in the basket and secured at the binding point by a wire pushed through slats at one end and covered by a generous blue gingham bow. Balance is important: the stems protrude over the back of the basket so that the arrangement is not top heavy. Although an impression of looseness is a key to success with cottage garden flowers, control must also be retained in the positioning and securing of the bouquet in the basket.

BRIDESMAIDS' WATERING CANS

The small bridesmaids carry little white enamelled cans, which have extenuated spouts like teapots and are half-filled with water. Because the fold-back lids open up only half of the top, room for the flowers is restricted. Delicate-petalled flowers – a lovely marriage of funnel-shaped aquilegia, purple, bell-like delphiniums and pink and red sweet williams – are arranged very simply within a framework of cow parsley. On each side of the handle, a blue gingham bow is attached with trailing white ribbons. Although the natural exuberance of cottage garden flowers seems to demand that they be used on an extravagant scale, it would be a pity to diminish the impact of the charming containers and the scale of the materials is carefully restrained.

Silver or copper watering cans would look just as beautiful, or the bridesmaids could carry the same flowers either spiralled in a posy or tied in a sheath and laid in a miniature trug that has been painted a pale pastel shade.

ARCH DECORATION

As quietly spectacular as it is romantic, the iron arch is wreathed with the wonderful pink climbing roses – a permanent feature of this garden – and bedecked with wedding flowers. Long branches of meadowsweet and Jacob's ladder are wired up the sides, along with delphiniums. Peonies and the purple michaelmas daisies are wired in, too; sprayed with water to keep them fresh, they should last four or five hours, depending on the weather.

For a less abundant – but longer-lasting – effect, the long-stemmed flowers can stand in buckets filled with water and chicken wire placed on either side of the arch. Near the curve of the arch, blocks of florist's plastic foam can be secured with chicken wire and the flowers arranged in that. However, the effect will not be quite as free and natural looking as here. Other dazzling displays can be created by training the flowers around a bare arch that has first been covered with beech leaves.

PALETTE OF FLOWERS

Aquilegia (columbine)
Saponaria
Sweet william
Godetia
Delphinium
Alchemilla mollis
Euphorbia
Peony
Michaelmas daisy

Jacob's ladder
Cow parsley
Meadowsweet

ARCH DECORATION
(left)
Cottage garden blooms wired on to a permanent arch create a lavish, sweet-smelling canopy. A temporary alternative would be to drive tall stakes into the ground to support flowers.

BRIDESMAIDS' WATERING CANS
(far left)
As a contrast to the cascading bouquet and exuberant arch, these little watering cans contain more restrained arrangements.

EXOTIC SPLASH

BRIDE'S BOUQUET
(left)
Spectacular Monstera deliciosa
*leaves provide an
extraordinary backdrop for
exotic azaleas and strelitzia.*

BRIDE'S BOUQUET
(left)
*The bright orange crest of the
strelitzia flower makes it easy
to understand how it acquired
its name of bird of paradise.*

*T*he idea of the flower as an exotic object is less familiar to us these days than it was just a few generations ago. Imagine the excitement our ancestors felt at seeing an anthurium for the first time, that strange, plastic-looking 'leaf' out of which grows a startling spathe, or a strelitzia, called a bird of paradise because it looks like an aristocratic, long-necked bird with exquisite markings. Both these plants are imports from tropical climes – the anthurium from South America and the strelitzia from South Africa – and both still seem exotic to most of us today.

But we have grown used to some plants that are equally striking. The familiar *Monstera deliciosa*, now an ubiquitous houseplant, was treated with awe when originally introduced from Mexico. Even the lavishly endowed rhododendron, which thrives in the temperate regions of the world and has thereby almost lost its 'exotic' status, comes originally from the foothills of the Himalayas. It was brought to Europe by adventurous eighteenth- and nineteenth-century botanists who scoured Asia for new species, bringing back at least 500, including azaleas. Smaller flowers with equally fascinating appearances and origins include the centaurea, native to the Caucasus, with its floppy yellow tuft on top, and the daisy-like gerbera from the Transvaal.

Used together, all these showy flowers create a big splash, a perfectly controlled spectacle of some of nature's brightest blooms. They have a vibrance and gaiety that cannot fail to bring a smile to the face of the stiffest father-in-law.

BRIDE'S BOUQUET

This colourful exuberance has been carefully scaled down in the bride's bouquet, and is replaced by an extraordinarily exotic but elegant combination of bird of paradise flowers and the big, perforated leaves of the *Monstera deliciosa* plant. The five strelitzia, which are left on their natural stems, are graded for position on the bouquet then trimmed accordingly. Since each stem is very heavy, it is supported by two long wires then double-leg mounted and taped (see page 134). The three stitched and mounted Monstera leaves are positioned around the focal flower (see page 133), under which a cluster of orange azaleas is recessed, providing a burst of colour when you look into the arrangement.

It is a very angular design which relies on balancing the size of the leaves and grading the length of the stems accurately. Although it looks simple, this is one of the more difficult arrangements to make, taking skill and experience. The only way to control the heavy materials is to wire them – the wires are then used to make the handle. It would be impossible to tie such a bouquet, because the stems are so thick and would make it very difficult to control the position of the flowers.

A similiar dramatic effect may be achieved by using anthurium with bear grass and three large leaves. But if the bride prefers something less stylized, a tied posy of red and yellow gerbera, sweet-smelling broom and golden rod would be colourful, quite exotic and certainly a splash.

PERGOLA DECORATION

The *pièce de résistance* at this wedding is the luxuriant, flower-decked, triple-arched pergola, a wonderful canopy that could be adapted with equal abandon for a chuppah. The iron arches are joined by three horizontal bars running the length of the pergola – one at the centre top, parallel to a bar on either side where the straight leg starts to curve to form the arch. It is a solid foundation for great 2 m (6 ft) tall branches of mauve rhododendron, which are tied on to create a dense canopy. The branches are laid from side to side, alternate branches facing with heads to the centre. They completely cover the top of the pergola, and are tied on to the side and central horizontal bars with gardening twine. This is an easy and effective way to decorate a pergola, with the generous rhododendron foliage and flowers supplemented by sturdy branches of yellow broom and golden rod (*Solidago*) pushed in between.

Near the top of each pole, three blocks of florist's plastic foam are taped on to the horizontal side bars and chicken wire is wrapped around to hold them in place. Within these, glorious displays of red, orange and yellow flowers are arranged. The flowers – pinky-red and orange gerberas, red anthurium, yellow centaurea, yellow broom and plumes of golden rod – sweep up, out to the sides and down in charming abundance. Three bird of paradise stems and rhododendron branches are attached to the base of each pole to mingle with the overflowing mass of flowers.

PERGOLA DECORATION
A dense canopy of exotic blooms is created on an iron pergola. This approach would be beautifully suited to a chuppah decoration for a Jewish wedding.

PALETTE OF FLOWERS

Gerbera
Anthurium
Centaurea
Strelitzia (bird of paradise)
Azalea
Yellow broom

Rhododendron
Golden rod (*Solidago*)
Monstera deliciosa

MIDSUMMER MEADOW

*E*verywhere you look in Provence, when summer is at its height, the meadows are clothed in tapestries of blues and yellows against deep, bright greens. Look southwards and the Mediterranean glimmers like silver and midnight-blue sapphires. Fields of buttercups, waist-high cow parsley left to run rampant and bluest cornflowers are round every corner. The air is heady with the perfume of the countryside – herbs crushed underfoot, newly cut crops, ripening fruit and the wonderful wild flowers.

Thriving in the meadows is a fine specimen of buttercup – not the typical short-stemmed one, but a variety that grows on long, strong stems, which hold up well in water. The pretty blue cornflowers are notable for their intensity, and the colour seems to spread out of their abundant lance-like petals. Less obvious, but equally charming, additions to these wedding flowers include the country-fresh cow parsley and the feathery light scabious with its wonderful pinky-blue flower – not unlike the cornflower – which unfurls to reveal a finely detailed centre.

JAM JAR DECORATIONS

Little attendants may prefer carrying tadpoles in their jam jars, but the adult onlookers will admire the wonderful casualness of pretty flowers in water. First of all, a length of cord is wound under the rim of the jar and tightly knotted at the side, then one end is continued over the top to make a handle and secured at the opposite side.

Cow parsley is used for the outline, and cornflowers, buttercups, scabious and white brodiaea are arranged in it. Although the jars are very simple to do and have a feeling of immediacy, the flowers should be carefully arranged rather than just pushed into the jars as children might do. Restricting the arrangement to buttercups and cow parsley would have been quite a charming alternative, or it could be all cow parsley – or even tadpoles.

PERFECT PASTURES
(left),
brimful with buttercups.

PALETTE OF FLOWERS

Buttercup
Brodiaea
Cornflower
Cow parsley
Scabious
Meadowsweet
Nigella
Golden rod *(Solidago)*

BRIDE'S POSY
(right)
Blue and yellow, one of nature's most striking schemes and a combination which inspired the peerless colourist Claude Monet, dominate in this loose posy.

GARLAND
(far right)
Buttercups and cornflowers – two of the most evocative flowers of the meadows – continue the blue and yellow theme in a garland of meadowsweet flowers.

BRIDE'S CORSAGE AND POSY

On her bodice, the bride wears a posy-type corsage. Made of wired buttercups and delicate white brodiaea, it is tightly spiralled (see page 133).

Blue and yellow dominate in the posy she carries. The basic outline of the posy is made with spiralled stems of cow parsley, its lacy clusters of cream flowers providing fullness and bulk. The cornflowers and the buttercups are threaded through, along with the lovely white brodiaea with its tiny bell-like flowers that look like miniature agapanthus. The posy, which is about 50 cm (20 in) across, is loose and very light, as if the bride had just gathered it up as she wandered through the meadows.

With these flowers, the effect is charmingly unstructured. As an alternative, the bride could carry a large trug filled with a loose tied bouquet. These are transient summer blooms and, for a longer life, the posy or bouquet should be left in water until the last possible moment.

GARLAND

The banqueting table is covered in a white cloth and the front swagged with muslin caught up at the corners and in the centre. The flowing lines of the muslin are emphasized by a garland of delicate meadowsweet flowers made in two crescent-shaped lengths. Light, frothy nigella, sprigs of cow parsley, cornflowers and fern are bound into loose, fairly long-stemmed bunches – about six bunches are needed for each length – and tied on to a main stay wire of gardening twine so that the garland is fatter in the middle than at the sides (see page 141). Some bunches are mixed, some are restricted to just one material. After the garland has been attached to the table, the buttercups and extra flowers and foliage are pushed in, adding to the loose, natural effect.

Because these flowers are so delicate, they should be left in water for at least four hours before the garland is made. Once tied into bunches, they can be put back into water and bound together to make the garland at the last moment.

FLOWER POT AND URN DECORATIONS

Three old flower pots are stacked at each of the three points where the garland is caught up on the front of the table. Each pot is lined with plastic and a small piece of florist's plastic foam, in which cow parsley and buttercups (the latter wired together in groups of three or four) are arranged to tumbling effect. The flowers should be sprayed with water.

Elegant weathered urns on either side of the gate are visions of white and yellow. Lined and filled with florist's foam, which is wedged in level with the rims and covered with chicken wire, the urns make handsome containers for abundant displays of loosely arranged cow parsley, masses of long-stemmed buttercups and golden rod (*Solidago*), subtly enhanced by a little pale blue-white nigella.

FLOWER POTS
(below)
AND URN DECORATIONS
(right)
*Bright buttercups spill out of
old flower pots, while stately
urn decorations add a note of
calm elegance.*

OLD-FASHIONED ROSES

BRIDE'S BOUQUET
(left)
The natural, pre-Raphaelite look of the bride's posy owes much to the combination of different-sized and -coloured roses. Using just one type of rose with saponaria – the moss rose, perhaps – would have a more formal effect.

ROSE PETAL CONFETTI
(left)
The rose is surely the most romantic of all flowers, throughout the centuries singled out by poets and painters as an emblem of beauty.

'O, my Love's like a red, red rose/That's newly sprung in June,' wrote the poet Robert Burns. The rose is the universal symbol of true love and giving roses is an expression of feeling which everyone understands. The choice of old-fashioned roses for wedding flowers must surely be one of the most classical of themes, and yet one which is rarely exploited.

Rose petals are strong and satin-like, yet fragrant and delicately coloured – and they may be crinkly or floppy, compact or cup-shaped. The pink shades of the old-fashioned roses used in these arrangements are truly wonderful: the palest tea-rose pink, orangey-pink, soft yellow edged with pink, pinky-mauve, deep dusky pink and a reddish pink put on a wonderful display. Mixing these closely related colours is even more successful when different varieties – and therefore different shapes, sizes and forms – are combined. Some are flat, others are layered in a tight spiral; some are large and full, others are in tight buds. The arrangements are a wonderful illustration of the charming effects which can be achieved by the massing of one type of flower which has within itself sufficient contrasts and gradations of texture, colour and shape. A mass of soft colour does need some definition, however, with a background against which to display the fragile looks and myriad forms of the flowers. The natural accompaniment to roses are their own ovate leaves and they have been used here to accentuate the subtle tones and shapes of the flowers. The only 'foreign' addition to the roses and their leaves is a white saponaria, which has wispy stems and is similar in effect to gypsophila but with slightly larger flowerheads.

BRIDE'S BOUQUET

The lovely looseness of the bouquet carried by the bride is a light counterpoint to the lavishness of her wonderful garland headdress. Roses left on natural stems, along with their foliage, give it a freer, lighter appearance. The hand-tied posy (see page 136) is round and the stems are spiralled, a technique which works particularly well with roses because they have very strong stems. Some of the flowers are recessed (see page 133), which provides a feeling of depth, and the sugared almond colours of the roses are beautifully enhanced by sprigs of white saponaria.

PALETTE OF FLOWERS

Gallica roses
Bourbon roses
Briar roses
Moss roses
Saponaria

Rose leaves
Ivy

BRIDESMAID'S HEADDRESS
(left)
The bridesmaid's headdress complements beautifully that of the bride, but is on a scale more suited to a small attendant.

BRIDE'S HEADDRESS
(right)
The Romans were passionate about roses and the classical look of this headdress is reinforced by the laurel-like rose leaves.

BRIDE'S HEADDRESS

The classical charm of the bride's headdress is underlined by the way in which so many roses are used close together, creating a wonderfully opulent effect. The very dense crown of magnificent blooms – the ancient French Gallica roses, with their delicate pink peppermint stripes, purple moss roses, tightly coiled white Bourbon roses, and carmine-pink wild briar roses – is wildly romantic.

Such a garland contains about 30 or 40 roses, making it rather expensive, particularly since it is made with full-blown old-fashioned roses, which may be difficult – but not impossible – to obtain. More and more florists are buying such roses directly from private country gardens. It may be cheaper, however, to buy flowering rose bushes, or the flowers could come directly from your own, or from a generous friend's, rose garden.

The stem of each rose is cut to about 4 cm (1½ in). An appropriate gauge wire is pushed horizontally through the base of the flowerhead then bent down and wound around the natural stem of the flower to create a false stem (see page 134). This should then be taped. This is a rather delicate operation, particularly for the Gallica roses, which have layers of fragile petals like flaky pastry and have a tendency to drop. The buds and smaller spray roses are wired in groups for a greater impact, then wired on to the individual blooms to create the headdress. The only subtle additions required to complete the effect are little clusters of wired and mounted (see page 134) rose leaves.

BRIDESMAID'S HEADDRESS

The bridesmaid's headdress is more simple to make: lush green ivy trails are wound around a main stay wire, and roses and rose leaves are concentrated towards the front of the garland (see page 138). The effect is charming on a small attendant and, fittingly, it echoes but does not upstage the bride's fuller headdress.

GARLAND

The bridesmaid and page boy carry between them a garland dripping with roses. It is based on a double length of gardening twine around which ivy trails have been wound. Small bunches or individual roses – graded according to size – have been wired on, starting with the smaller blooms at each end and using fuller bunches towards the middle, producing a crescent shape (see page 141). To make each ribbon handle, loop a length of ribbon in half, then double-leg mount and stitch it (see page 134). This loop is then wired to the end of the garland and the join disguised by a ribbon bow (see page 135). Here, a wide, deep pink taffeta ribbon has been used, to enhance the lovely tints and paler pinks of the roses.

**HEADDRESSES AND
GARLAND**
*(right and below)
Full bunches of the largest,
most opulent roses are
concentrated in the centre of
this magnificent garland to
create a gloriously perfumed
crescent of blooms.*

SUMMER WHITES

MESSING ABOUT ON
THE RIVER
(left)
*Edwardian dress and an
antique rowing boat set just
the right tone for this relaxed
summer wedding, reminiscent
of an elegant turn-of-the-
century boating party.*

*P*ure white, dazzling blooms stand out against a verdant background, their whiteness reflecting all the rays from the sun. This classic summer wedding is composed on the theme of white and green, as timely and romantic as floating down the river on a gently drifting boat. It is a particularly seasonal choice, the only time of the year when such a monochromatic scheme is really successful. In winter, for example, cream and a touch of pink are needed to supplement white, otherwise the flowers look too harsh and cold. But in summer, when the sun is blazing, white flowers create a feeling of coolness and simple sophistication.

The summer garden offers a profusion of white flowers. In these designs stock and scabious are used in large quantities, as well as sweet william, marguerites, saponaria and philadelphus, but sweet peas and peonies, delphiniums and larkspur, roses and irises would have been just as suitable.

HOOPS AND HATS
(above)
*A graceful hoop and a wittily
decorated hat are charmingly
fitting arrangements for a little
bridesmaid and a sailor-suited
page boy.*

BRIDE'S BOUQUET

The sparkling whiteness of the flowers stands out in the bride's bouquet, offset by the luxurious green of the foliage, and the delicacy of the individual flowers is emphasized by the generous scale. This wonderful tied shower bouquet (see page 136) is a perfumed composition of long-stemmed white scabious, stock with its heady scent and copious flowerheads, clusters of white sweet william. and the very summery saponaria; only the centre of the almost leafless scabious flower, which is daisy-like and usually a pinky-blue colour, is slightly off-white.

The basic outline is made from branches of philadelphus (mock orange). Although the stems have buds and some fully opened, sweet-smelling flowers, the philadelphus is used more for its foliage. The heart-shaped leaves are a lush, almost black-green colour and look matt rather than glossy. The stems are quite twiggy, so the ends can be stripped and they should be left in water for a few hours before use.

This is quite a heavy bouquet containing a lot of dense materials, and it needs to be held with both hands. To achieve such a full shape – from the side it curves out like a bass clef – full advantage is taken of the natural flow of the flowers and foliage; the philadelphus, for example, is long and curved and has been used to define the length and sweep of the bouquet. Stock, too, is often an interesting shape, while scabious has long stems, and so the natural length of both flowers should be used. One important technique to remember when making this lovely shower shape is to recess some of the flowers, which fills out the bouquet and creates the illusion of depth (see page 133).

The same materials could be wired, on their natural stems, into a smaller shower bouquet or a round posy, possibly adding a lily or rose as a focal flower to give it body. Using different foliage would change the look of the bouquet. If the bride wanted lime green, for example, a good choice would be *Alchemilla mollis* with its palmate leaves.

PALETTE OF FLOWERS

Stock
Scabious
Sweet william
Marguerite
Saponaria
Philadelphus (mock orange)
Alchemilla mollis
Loosestrife *(Lythrum)*

**PAGE BOY'S HOOP AND
BRIDE'S BOUQUET**
(left)
*The page boy's hoop is simply
decorated with marguerite
foliage and flowers.*

BRIDE'S BOUQUET
(far left)
*The bride's arrangement
seems almost a continuation
of the exuberant white rose
bushes behind her. Held from
the side, the bouquet displays
an elegant sweeping curve.*

DECORATED HATS
AND HOOPS
(far right and right)
A bunch of jauntily arranged
marguerites are the perfect
decoration for a mischievous
little attendant's straw boater.
The bridesmaid's hat is simply
decorated with three wired
scabious blooms, echoing the
more formal use of the
scabious flowers in her
beautifully composed hoop.

DECORATED HATS AND HOOPS

The little attendants in sailor clothes hold on tightly to their jaunty straw boaters. One is decorated with a bunch of marguerites, the other with lace ribbon and three wired scabious pushed into the bow at the back.

The children just resist the temptation to trail their pretty hoops over the side of the boat. The page boy's hoop is very simply decorated, to avoid damaging delicate male sensibilities. A white metal hoop, about 50 cm (20 in) in diameter, is covered with the daisy-like marguerite, which is left on a fairly long stem (about 20 cm (8 in) in length); each bloom has two or three little flowerheads and lots of lovely, silvery grey foliage. The flowers, arranged in a cartwheel pattern, are bound individually on to the hoop with silver reel wire (see page 138).

The bridesmaid's hoop is very structured. It is made in the same way as a garland headdress (see page 138), little bunches of *Alchemilla mollis*, sweet william and loosestrife (*Lythrum*) and individual scabious flowers are wired then taped on to the hoop in a regular pattern (see page 138). The materials are directed so that they face the front; the top section of the hoop is left bare and decorated with two long white ribbons which are tied in bows so that they trail down.

White-on-white has a grace and subtlety all of its own. And the interplay of white and green is made more interesting in these designs by the introduction of different greens: a darkish green in the bride's bouquet, a lime tint in the little bridesmaid's flowers, and a silvery, sage green in the page boy's hoop add depth and contrast.

WOODLAND ROMANCE

'What angel wakes me from my flowery bed?' asks Titania in Shakespeare's *A Midsummer Night's Dream.* These wonderful woodland woodland flowers and leaves have all the grace of the wild flowers of midsummer upon which Titania slept.

The profusion of greenery found in the woods at the height of summer creates a symphony of light and dark, and includes deep emeralds and dark blue-greens, clear colours and light lime shades, sage and silvery tones and pale grey-greens. In these wedding flowers, mixing matt with gloss, tissue-paper thin with coarse, feathery with palmate, and adding in unopened buds, nut cases and seed wings, reproduces the magnificent variety found in nature. Many of the blooms still grow in the wild, as they did in Shakespeare's day, but they are also available commercially.

MIDSUMMER MAGIC
This midsummer wedding is charged with the ethereal, bewitching beauty which cloaks woodlands at this time of year.

BRIDESMAID'S HEADDRESS
(right)
Although it is in fact carefully constructed, the garland headdress looks as if it has just been gathered from its woodland setting. The delicate pink foxgloves are the main flowers in the arrangement. Their name – from the Old English Foxes glofa – *is delightfully appropriate to this magical woodland setting with the image it conjures up of mischievous foxes with petal gloves.*

BRIDESMAID'S HEADDRESS
(right)
Clusters of many different woodland materials – from foxglove and monkshood heads to sycamore wings and beech nuts – are united by ivy wound around the completed garland. The white, hooded flowers of monkshood are charming, but be careful when handling them as the plant is poisonous.

BRIDESMAID'S HEADDRESS

The beauty of the woodlands is displayed in full in the wonderful garland headdress created for a small bridesmaid. Groups of sycamore wings, and of young beech leaves and nuts, are wired together (see page 138), as are pretty bunches of elderflower, of monkshood and of lady's mantle. Small fern fronds which grow on the floor of the woodlands are stripped and wired together in clusters. Because the pink foxglove heads are soft and hollow, they are more difficult to handle. A silver wire bent in half is twisted at the top to make a loop, then pushed down the throat of the flower so that it lodges in the neck; to secure it firmly, the wired flowerhead is mounted on to another silver wire then taped.

From these beautiful woodland materials, a garland is made by wiring one bunch on to another, alternating the different elements and distributing the foxgloves in little clusters throughout. It is important to take into account the size of the head: a child's usually ranges from 47.5-52.5 cm (19-21 in), an adult's from 50-55 cm (20-22 in). When the headdress is completed, ivy trails are wound around it.

Extravagant in size and effect, the headdress is a profusion of greens and tiny pale flowerheads, with the prickly beech nuts and knobbly sycamore wings adding texture, and the pinkish tinges in the sycamore echoing the colour of the foxgloves. It is a large headdress which literally crowns the head and commands attention.

BRIDE'S BOUQUET

But, as is fitting, it is the bride who steals the day with her spectacular bouquet. It is a glorious showcase for the tall foxglove, whose spikes of tubular flowers are seen at their best used full length. The lovely white monkshood flower, which grows in racemes (clusters) like grapes on tall stems, adds necessary lightness. Take care, however, when handling monkshood as the plant and flowers are poisonous.

The bouquet is a tied sheaf (see page 136) which is built up from an ouline of ivy trails and long fern fronds. Deep green beech leaves and their young woody fruits, branches of flowering elder and the other materials already used in the headdress are included and full advantage is taken of their natural shapes and direction of growth.

Handling such a large amount of materials can be difficult, but by spiralling the flowers and foliage a narrow binding point is created (see page 136). The stems balance the weight of the front of the bouquet and, because they are angled from the binding point, allow the bouquet to be held easily, either in two hands or carried over the arm. For something this size, the best approach is to attach gardening twine to the first bunches of materials used and bind it round group by group. This allows you to angle the material into the desired shape whilst still being able to hold it.

URN ARRANGEMENT

An equally profusive woodland harvest is arranged in a classical urn. A bucket placed in the urn is filled with chicken wire and water. Then long fern fronds, great stems of foxgloves, and the slender stalks of loosestrife (*Lythrum*) with its densely packed, star-shaped purple flowerheads, are distributed and long pieces of blue-green ivy trail down, as they would naturally.

Because they are on such a large scale, these arrangements may not appeal to everyone. To achieve a similar feel on a smaller scale, a tied posy of monkshood and fern with beech nuts work well filled in with a soft starry mass of elderflowers and short trails of ivy. The foxgloves are too long to use on their natural stem and are better left out. The bridesmaid could carry a little basket of the same flowers or a small tied posy of beech nuts and leaves, branches of elderflower and feathery fern fronds.

The secret of handling these wonderful woodland flowers successfully is to keep the arrangements very simple. The sheer exuberance of the materials means they lend themselves naturally to being used on an extravagant scale and by using the flowers and foliage on their natural stems and exploiting their full length and natural directions of growth, full advantage can be taken of their inherent drama.

PALETTE OF FLOWERS

Foxglove
Elderflower
Monkshood

Lady's mantle
Fern
Ivy
Loosestrife *(lythrum)*
Sycamore wings
Beech leaves
Beech nuts

ELIZABETHAN HERBAL

*S*weet smells of herbs are released as Elizabethan courtiers, bedecked in heavy brocades, gold chains and pearls, sweep past ankle-high hedges of thyme and lavender that have been trimmed into elaborate knots or elongated diamonds, surrounded by gravelled paths and graceful statuary. The colours of the leaves and flowers are softly muted – gentle golds, dusky pinks, strange mauves, yellowy creams, and sage greens – as in faded tapestries, and everything appears to be in miniature, made up of tiny stitches. In its time, the knot garden held all the secrets of the alchemist as well as those of the master chef.

BRIDE'S HEADDRESS

The finely etched detail of the Elizabethan knot garden is repeated in the bride's headdress, which is attached to the comb that secures her veil. It is made in a crescent shape, broadened across the forehead and narrowed at the sides.

Texture and contrasting shapes play an important role. Small pieces of yarrow picked off the main head, spiky lavender flowers, tiny round thistle heads of 'Blue Ribbon' echinops, a couple of *Hebe* flowers with their foliage, flat-leaved continental parsley, sprigs of thyme and sage leaves are all wired into little bunches. Yellow and purple pansies, their stems cut to about 1.5 cm (½ in) and then wired and mounted, are used individually.

To make the headdress, the bunches are wired on to a stiff stay wire, the shape being built up gradually (see page 138). Securing the headdress to the comb requires a delicate touch, because in this case the veil is already attached. Silver reel wire is stitched through the stay wire, wound carefully through the back of the wired bunches, then around the top of the comb. This will keep the headdress secure, even if the bride folds the upper layer of her veil over her face.

BRIDE'S HEADDRESS
(left),
inspired by the embroidered
caps of Elizabethan women.

TUSSIE MUSSIES

Smaller tussie mussies, little tied posies of sweet-smelling herbs and flowers, are carried by the three bridesmaids. The tight, delicate-looking spiralled posies – no more than 15 cm (6 in) in diameter – are full of surprises.

Each of the three is different, but the construction is the same – spiralled in the hand (see page 133) from a central flower, tied with gardening twine, the stems trimmed and the tussie finished with an embroidered ribbon edged with mauve velvet. One is all deep purples and reds, centred around a cluster of old-fashioned primula flowers surrounded by a ring of thyme, then lavender; next, the 'Blue Ribbon' echinops thistle is alternated with little bunches of flat-leaved parsley, and the tussie is edged with red sage. A pinky-white 'Apothecary's' rose is the focal point of the second posy, and is circled by white *Hebe*, the echinops thistles, thyme, variegated thyme and feathery, spherical chive flowers. The third is all yellows and whites, with a pansy in the centre among yarrow, the tiny, daisy-like feverfew, white *Hebe*, golden sage and variegated thyme.

NAPKIN DECORATION
(below),
made from simple twines of
daisy-like feverfew.

TUSSIE MUSSIES
(right)
were traditionally carried to
ward off unpleasant smells.

PALETTE OF FLOWERS

Yarrow (*Achillea*)
Lavender
'Blue Ribbon' echinops
Hebe
Flat-leaved parsley
Thyme
Variegated thyme
Red sage
Golden sage
Marjoram
Chive
Feverfew
Pansy
Primula
'Apothecary's' rose

CANDELABRUM
DECORATION
(right)
*Imposing candelabra
decorated in this way with
fragrant garlands of flowers
and foliage could adorn the
dining table at an Elizabethan
inspired wedding. Feverfew,
which is combined here with
sprigs of continental parsley,
has been used for centuries in
herbal medicine and featured
in poltices and concoctions
designed to cure melancholy.*

POMANDER
(right)
*The herbal pomander was
another device carried in
Elizabethan times to perfume
the air. In addition to their
delightful fragrance, the short
stems and densely packed
leaves of many herbs make
them a particularly suitable
choice for the base foliage of a
pomander. As well as being
carried by the bride and
bridesmaid, these sweet-
smelling pomanders could
also decorate a house or
reception room.*

CANDELABRUM DECORATION

Draped over the candelabrum is a garland of fragrant foliage. Feverfew left on the stem and sprigs of continental parsley are wired on to each other with very fine silver reel wire to make a loose trail, which in turn is wound in and out of the candle holders. Towards the base, more foliage has been added to give a feeling of opulence. The garland will last two or three hours if sprayed with water.

POMANDER

The Elizabethan street was not the most hygienic or fragrant of places, and people carried pomanders and muffs made of sweet-smelling herbs to perfume the evil air. This bride has a wonderful pomander of fresh herbs and old-fashioned flowers – for visual effect rather than health reasons. The finished flower ball is about 30 cm (12 in) in diameter. Its base is a piece of florist's plastic foam, which has been rounded at the corners, then covered with chicken wire. A wide purple satin ribbon edged with gold is looped through the chicken wire to make a handle before the pomander is covered with flowers and herbs, which have 5-7.5 cm (2-3 in) stems (see page 139).

Sprigs of thyme, dense pointed spikes of white and mauve *Hebe* flowers and soft-stemmed marjoram wired into little bunches are used all over the base. Complementing these small, delicate-looking plants are two sages – a red variety and golden sage. More prominent are the clusters of tiny mustard-yellow yarrow (*Achillea*) flowers, the strong colour of which is balanced by the soft, cobwebby effect of the 'Blue Ribbon' echinops thistle, with its purply green stem.

$\mathcal{A}$UTUMN

As the year mellows and matures
after the extravagances of summer,
nature gathers up all her powers for a
crescendo of ever-deepening colour
and richness. Branches hang heavy
with burnished fruits; the produce of
the fields ripens in the last golden
rays of sunshine; and in the
lengthening shadows flowers and
foliage blaze with fiery colour.

HARVEST THANKSGIVING

*N*ature produces an inferno of colour as summer draws into autumn. As the autumn leaves turn to russet, copper, gold and bronze, the gardens, fields and orchards produce their riches. The honey-coloured sheaves of wheat are cut, baskets of apples and pears are gathered, berries ripen and the last ears of golden corn are harvested.

The sheaf of wheat has been the traditional symbol of the harvest since Egyptian times. Deftly braided wheat ornaments decorate country homes during festivals celebrated all over Europe and North America, and mounds of pumpkins and cauliflowers, cabbages and beans are piled up in churches as the congregations offer thanks for a good harvest. For this charming country wedding, a feature is made of the sheaves of wheat, in the bouquet and the pew ends. The orange-gold palette of autumn is celebrated with 'Aalsmere Gold' roses and tiny 'Enchantment' lilies. The abundance of the harvest is represented by bunches of baby radishes, carrots and turnips, and the fruits of the orchard by russet-coloured pears and deep red berries.

URN ARRANGEMENT
(left)
*A mass of orange-gold flowers
tumble from the hay.*

GERBERA
(below)
*Honey-coloured wheat offsets
the gerbera's fiery red.*

BRIDE'S BOUQUET

The bride carries her hand-tied bouquet (see page 136) over the arm, as if she has just gathered it from the fields. A very simple, but effective combination of wheat, 'Connecticut King' lilies and 'Aalsmere Gold' roses is used. The stems of the individual flowers and thin bunches of wheat (the bouquet would take hours to make if the wheat was treated separately) are arranged in the hand. They should be spiralled (see page 136), with the flowers at the front, so that the arrangement has a sheaf-like, rather than bunched, effect, and the wheat and lilies are used to give it length. A simply tied, flowing ribbon, attached at the binding point, is in keeping with the loose, rippling feel of the bouquet and adds to the impression of length.

GARLAND HEADDRESS

The bridesmaid's garland headdress is a veritable salad of autumn vegetables and blooms (see page 138). Baby radishes, carrots, beans and turnips are wired individually then wired into little bunches. The mushrooms are cut in half and two pieces of thin silver wire are pushed into the rounded back then stitched (see page 134) to give them support. The baby vegetables, which work so well in this kind of arrangement, giving a feeling of depth, are taped with florist's tape on to the base of the headdress, which is formed by a main stay wire, along with curly leafed parsley and 'Aalsmere Gold' roses. Virtually any small vegetables can be used in this way, adding a more unexpected element, but one that is entirely in keeping with the harvest theme.

BRIDE'S BOUQUET
(above left)
Wheat, the traditional symbol of the harvest, is incorporated in the bride's bouquet and used to create a sheaf-like effect.

GARLAND HEADDRESS
(above)
The rounded shape of tiny vegetables such as radishes, turnips and mushrooms is echoed in that of the 'Aalsmere Gold' roses.

POMANDER
(left)
Silken roses are enhanced by the texture of antique lace.

POMANDERS

The small bridesmaids carry fragrant and colourful pomanders. The base is a small piece of florist's plastic foam which is wrapped in chicken wire (see page 139). The ribbon loop is attached first, its two ends stitched together with silver wire, which is then twisted firmly round the chicken wire. At this point the pomanders should be hung up, making the distribution of the decoration easier. A lovely herby fragrance comes from parsley and thyme which are used to cover the whole surface of the balls. Firm-stemmed flowers – the roses and ranunculus in the more colourful pomander, and the orange 'Tap-toe' lilies used unaccompanied in the simpler arrangement – are pushed in unwired, along with various wired baby vegetables.

POMANDER
(left)
Ranunculus and 'Aalsmere Gold' roses are set against a background of fragrant thyme and parsley. Cranberries and baby vegetables, including turnips and radishes, add further to the delightfully contrasting textures.

POMANDERS
(above)
The harvest theme of abundance and extravagant colour is continued in these two pomanders. The simpler arrangement (right) uses only 'Tap-toe' lilies, but their orange petals, which graduate to a creamy yellow in the centre, provide rich variety within a single flower.

PALETTE OF FLOWERS

'Aalsmere Gold' rose
'Enchantment' lily
'Connecticut King' lily
Ranunculus
Gerbera
Chinese lantern *(physalis)*

Birch twigs
Corn
Parsley
Thyme
Turnip
Mushroom
Raddichio
Artichoke
Cauliflower
Cranberry
Red William pear
Radish
Green bean
Carrot

URN ARRANGEMENT

The great charm of the large arrangement is the happy profusion of colour, tumbling flowers and produce, set firmly in the farmyard. Based in a traditional Provençal ceramic pot (containing a bucket lined with plastic foam and chicken wire), which has been positioned on the hay-laden cart, the arrangement has been built up on a framework of birch twigs and features the yellow 'Connecticut King' lilies, orange 'Tap-toe' lilies, and red, daisy-like gerberas (see page 133). Pumpkins, squash and globe artichokes are piled up on the cart, among the hay and flowers, as if they have just been brought in from the fields.

A similar mass of flowers could be set on a pedestal in the church and surrounded by a still life of vegetables such as squash, aubergines, cauliflowers and cabbages. Alternatively these could be wired into the arrangement itself. Spectacular centrepieces for the wedding table can be created using fruit, vegetables and flowers. The lilies and roses would work particularly well, perhaps grouped in baskets and surrounded by baby vegetables. Squash and pumpkins lend themselves to something on a grander scale, perhaps in a pyramid-shaped arrangement or tumbling from large bowls on to a buffet or banqueting table. What matters is that the arrangement is generous in scope, giving the wonderful feeling of abundance that is the essence of harvest time.

PEW END

The bright lanterns of dried *physalis* (Chinese lanterns), which have the delicate appearance of wild flowers and deceptively strong stems, look like jewels among the wheat. These are tied together to make pew ends using the same method as for the bouquet. Once the sheaves are attached to the pew, varieties of baby radicchio, pears and globe artichokes are wired and pushed into the binding point; alternatively, they can be included in the sheaf, but this will not give such a stable result and restricts the options for positioning. The finishing touch is the cranberries, each berry wired individually then bound together in a group. The decorative pew end can be made the day before the wedding and will hold up well.

PEW END
(left)
The harvest motif is given glorious expression in a pew end arrangement which could have come straight from the fields. Such an arrangement could also decorate the stair rails of a house or poles of a marquee.

URN ARRANGEMENT
(far left)
Arrangements do not have to be confined to conventional sites. The hay-laden cart provides a wonderful backdrop for this loosely flowing composition.

PERFECT PASTELS

BRIDE'S BOUQUET
(left)
Pale creams, pinks and mauves may not be colours usually associated with autumn, but these delicate flowers introduce a touch of light gracefulness into an autumn day.

TABLE ARRANGEMENT
(left)
With its gentle dome shape, the table arrangement strikes a distinctive note, yet is low enough to be placed on a dining table.

The bride is often advised to choose seasonal flowers only, yet there are so many other interesting possibilities that might better suit the type of wedding she wants. Autumn is a time of gold, deep browns and russet reds. But there is another, paler, side to the season. The delicacy of these plants and flowers, the soft colours and the exquisiteness of the blooms, are associated more with spring and summer – yet all the materials used here are readily available in the autumn.

Among the flowers chosen for this wedding are several that bloom right through late summer and early autumn, including two types of rose – the delicate 'La Minuet' spray rose, which is a very pale pink, and the floribunda 'Iceberg' rose, with its distinctive pale yellow bloom – the 'Mona Lisa' alstroemerias (Peruvian lilies) with their twisted trumpet-shaped flowers, which are cream with a tinge of pink, and the lovely 'Iceland' poppies, whose petals are so delicate that they appear to be made of tissue paper. The yarrow plant flowers right through the late summer and into autumn, and only the grape hyacinth (muscari) is truly out of season, but readily available via the flower markets.

Although the colours are soft and spring-like, the use of deep creams, of pale yellows and a touch of pink warms up the arrangements. White flowers combined with the mauve of the grape hyacinth would have been too harsh a composition for a cold, blustery autumn day. But these elegant flowers exhibit a lovely honey-coloured glow and a timeless beauty. The clear green foliage of the alstroemerias, the tiny berries of the tree ivy and the small silver, furry leaves of *Senecio greyi*, a houseplant of New Zealand origin, are used sparingly and to great effect.

BRIDE'S BOUQUET

The bouquet designed for the bride is small and round, only about 25 cm (10 in) in diameter, and tied in a dome shape (see page 136). By spiralling the stems (see page 136), a wonderful tight bunch shape is created. The small, delicate flowers used – the roses, alstroemeria, the palest 'Iceland' poppies, grape hyacinths (muscari) and yarrow, a perennial herb – lend themselves very well to this technique. The colours are light and rather formal, and the shape is controlled yet very natural.

PALETTE OF FLOWERS

'La Minuet' spray rose
'Iceberg' rose
'Iceland' poppy
Grape hyacinth (muscari)
Senecio greyi
Alstroemeria

Yarrow
Berried ivy

TABLE ARRANGEMENT

The antique, criss-crossed wire basket holding the table arrangement is oval shaped and about 30 cm (12 in) long. Any container that is not water-tight or is particularly precious, like this one, should be protected by lining it with plastic or using a container inside (see page 142). Here, half a block of florist's plastic foam has been placed in a round container and the flowers then positioned in the foam. Continuing the theme of the bride's bouquet, it is a loose, gently domed arrangement that is designed to be seen from all sides, and would therefore be suitable for a drinks or dining table. Only one type of rose, the spray rose 'La Minuet', has been used, and a few stems of berried ivy have been added.

The success of this arrangement depends on the shape and the distribution of flowers. The outline is constructed first using the ivy and the grape hyacinths, the latter wired in bunches of five or six rather than individually. The other flowers, which are then distributed evenly throughout, do not need wiring, not even the poppies, whose stems, although not terribly strong, are quite stiff and therefore easy to push into the foam.

The very delicate, natural effect of the arrangement is achieved by the use of small, exquisite blooms and the *ad hoc* placing of the flowers. If the wedding feast is laid on small tables, the arrangement can easily be scaled down. And because these flowers are so soft and delicate, they may be placed on the cake table without overwhelming the cake.

Such flowers are designed for a small-scale wedding. Yet in a larger arrangement the same gentle effect need not be lost if similar care is taken to choose flowers whose colour and texture is in tune with the delicate tone. In the bouquet, for instance, the cream 'Mont Blanc' lily, with its star-shaped head, or the pale pink 'Apple Blossom' amaryllis, would look wonderful.

The overall effect of these pretty pastels is soft and formal, very different from the strong hues and country themes usually associated with autumn. These are flowers that lend themselves to sophisticated tables set with fine glass- and silverware, beautiful porcelain and heavy damask. Like the delicate little blooms, the small details are important in this overall picture of perfection.

TABLE ARRANGEMENT
*Antique silver complements
the pastel blooms.*

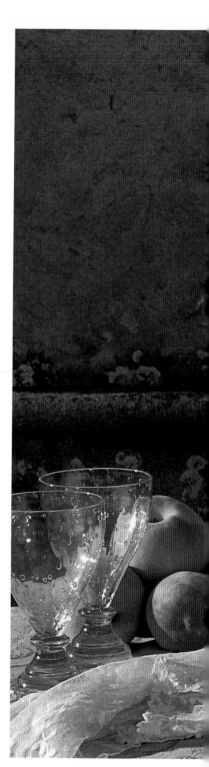

FOREST ENCHANTMENT

*D*eep in the forest, among the russet shades of autumn, the evergreens take on a shadowy depth and mystery all of their own. Where the sunlight penetrates down to the forest floor, wondrous patches of wild flowers and rambling roses flourish, their brilliance intensified by the unexpectedness of their presence in the darkness. Brambles and shrubs are heavy with berries, acorns fall from the oaks, and fungi sprout out of the damp earth. The fruits of the forest are gathered for food, made into cordials and wines, and used for decoration. The warmth of their colours compensates for the cold weather that is approaching.

Restricting the colours of the flowers for this wedding to reds and cream, and using dark green and silvery foliage, provides both richness and restraint, a sense of shadowy mystery. The number of flowers is limited but well chosen, allowing much to be made of the deep reds of the velvety 'Red Ace' spray rose (which opens out to display a creamy yellow centre) and the anemones, the cream statice, and the lovely 'Vicki Brown' rose whose petals are cream on the outside and red inside.

The foliage plays an important part in these arrangements, which is particularly useful at this time of year when expense and limited availability restrict one's choice of fresh flowers and when the wealth of foliage on offer is particularly spectacular. The glossy green of the tree ivy, the veined *hedera* (ivy) that displays all the transience of the season as it varies from shades of green through to golden-tinted browns, and the silvery green of the rosemary work beautifully together. Much is made of the play between the glossiness of the tree ivy and rose leaves, and the matt texture of the rosemary leaves. There are other contrasts too, such as the dark berries of the tree ivy against the pink-red of rosehips and the crimson hawthorn berries.

BRIDE'S BOUQUET
*A wonderful tangle of deep red
flowers and lush foliage spills
out of the wicker basket in
which it is carefully secured.*

BRIDE'S BOUQUET
(right)
Trails of ivy used in different lengths are central to the cascading effect of the bouquet and the wide, star-shaped leaves contrast beautifully with the delicate catkins and old man's beard.

GARLAND HEADDRESS
AND
BRIDESMAID'S BASKET
(right)
Individual clusters of woodland material make up the garland, which is united by twines of ivy. A similar technique is used for the bridesmaid's basket which echoes the wicker trug carried by the bride.

BRIDE'S BOUQUET

Autumn is a time for gathering the fruits of the forest, and the bride carries a low trug full of flowers. Arranged in the hand and wired into the basket at the binding point (see page 140), the bouquet is constructed on a framework of catkins, ivy and rosemary, into which the flowers – the 'Vicki Brown' roses, red anemones, *Mahonia japonica*, rosehips and old man's beard – are pushed and angled to give a profile (see page 133) to the bouquet. The main flower is the rose, with the anemones restricted to a transitional role (see page 133). Foliage is integral to the arrangement and even though only two varieties of flower are used, the overall effect is very rich and lush.

Because the bouquet is weighty, it must be carefully balanced, for visual as well as practical reasons. This is why stems have been left on. The successful proportions are straightforward – two-thirds of the whole arrangement are in the basket, and half of this is taken up by the stems – with the result that the flowers look as if they have just been picked, tumbling, as they do, over the edge of the basket with a wonderful cascading effect. It also means that the bride can carry the basket quite naturally and easily.

GARLAND HEADDRESS

The garland that adorns the bridesmaid's head is made of little bunches of plant material, which are bound on to each other rather than on to a base, then ivy trails are woven around the clusters (see page 138) in the finished headdress. Each cluster varies: roses and hawthorn berries are bunched together, beside a cluster of statice and berried ivy, or, perhaps a cluster of spray roses and statice. The garland may be preserved after the wedding day – the best method is to hang it up in a warm room or place it in silica gel (see page 135). The berries may shrivel up but the headdress as a whole will hold up well.

BRIDESMAID'S BASKET

The bridesmaid continues the gathering theme by carrying a garlanded basket, made in the same way as the headdress, with little wired bunches of flowers and foliage. These are stitched (see page 133) on to the edge of the basket, using a very fine silver reel wire, and ivy trails are then wound around them and over the handle in the way ivy naturally grows and entwines itself. The basket can be filled with nuts or berries, or perhaps petals or confetti.

PALETTE OF FLOWERS

'Red Ace' spray rose
'Vicki Brown' spray rose
Anemone
Statice

Mahonia
Trailing ivy
Berried ivy

Rosehip
Hawthorn berries
Rosemary
Old man's beard

SWAG
A grand sweep of luxuriant reds and greens adorns the church door. In this arrangement the dominant colours are offset by the delicate cream hues of statice.

SWAG

Hung decoratively on a door or wall, the swag-shaped arrangement is tied from a binding point on the side rather than at the back or the top (see page 141). It has been designed to take advantage of the natural shape of the foliage, and has been built up with a flat back and carefully shaped profile. There is a concentration on foliage combined with statice and on the careful placing of red anemones and 'Vicki Brown' roses.

Tying does take skill. An alternative method is to use a plastic 'shovel' (available from florist suppliers) filled with soaked plastic foam as a base, into which the foliage and flowers are pushed. However, this limits the size of the arrangement: heavy material will eventually fall out as the foam dries and crumbles. A more complicated, but far stronger, technique – and one particularly suitable for dried flowers – is to bind small bunches of material on to a central rope or wire. The trick lies in varying the length and the profile of the bunches to achieve a natural-looking effect.

The edge of the wedding table can be garlanded with swags, or the table itself decorated with baskets similar to those carried by the bridesmaids, and filled to overflowing with the fruits of the forest, with cranberries and branches of blackberries, loosely arranged flowers and piles of nuts. The overall flavour is one of wild bounty.

GARLAND HEADDRESS
(above)
*A perfect circle of forest fruits
and foliage evokes all the
riches of the season.*

MEDIEVAL MAGNIFICENCE

BRIDE'S BOUQUET
(left)
*The sumptuous flowing effect
of the hand-tied bouquet is
entirely in keeping with the
opulent medieval tone.*

GLORIOSA LILY
(left)
*With its extravagant array of
colours and crinkled petals
reminiscent of crushed velvet,
the gloriosa, or 'glory', lily more
than lives up to its name.*

The rich, deep colours and textures of velvets and satins, damasks and silks, the fine detail of tapestries and medieval illuminations, and the graceful tracery of the great Gothic buildings evoke images of medieval passions and courtly love. The singular notes of the mandolin and lute pierce the air, which is heavy with the fragrance of rose petals mixed with exotic spices.

The choice of the strong colours seen in medieval manuscripts and tapestries for an occasion traditionally thought to require pastels or even white is a bold one, and it is this use of colour that gives such pleasurable harmony to the arrangements. The almost fabric-like textures of the various flowers, and the juxtaposition of dense purples with rich reds and golds, create a feeling of opulence that is satisfying both texturally and visually. The bride might wear cream satin, silk organza or handmade lace, or she may choose something less conventional but equally medieval, such as rich velvet or brocade and shades of peacock green, ruby red or deep purple.

On the medieval wedding table, fruit, vegetables, nuts and berries can all be used to enormous effect, piled up in mounds on tables, tumbling from baskets and vases and wired into groups in large displays. Pyramids of fruit and flowers with gilded dried globe artichokes and walnuts look stunning amongst huge beeswax candles. Trails of ivy and old man's beard can be swagged along the fronts of tables, and caught up with opulent, theatrical bows of wide silk or rich velvet ribbon. The accent is on drama and luxury on this most celebratory of days.

BRIDE'S BOUQUET

The bouquet is hand tied, a method of construction that allows the flowers to appear loosely placed, although in fact they are carefully controlled: a wired bouquet in which the flowers are left on their stems rather than cut off at the head would achieve the same flowing effect (see page 136). The wavy-edged petals of the parrot tulips and gloriosa lilies lend a delicacy to the strong hues, the blown spray roses have a feeling of abandon, and the strong-lined trumpet-shaped amaryllis is positioned deep in the bouquet to give visual depth to the composition. Restricting the use of the purple anemones balances the arrangement, and rosemary and mahonia provide a spiky texture in contrast to the flat leaves of trailing ivy.

TABLE ARRANGEMENT

The table arrangement illustrated is made in a low round wooden bowl and is designed to sit against a wall or in a corner, perhaps on a drinks or buffet table (see page 142). In order to attain these graceful lines, blocks of florist's plastic foam are built up quite high above the rim of the bowl and secured by chicken wire, which allows the flowers to be angled to create a tumbling effect. The red and gold of the gloriosa lily and the parrot tulip draw the eye through the arrangement, and are striking against the dark foliage, and particularly against the glossy camelia leaves. The purple anemones and spray roses are used as the transitional flowers (see page 133) providing visual interest.

It is unwise to make an arrangement so tall that the guests cannot see through it to talk to one another, but the flowers can be raised above their heads – for example, on lightweight metal pedestals placed on the table and filled with flowers trailing down and around the stand. Gloriosa plants, the stems of which grow in long tendrils, are wonderful for decorating on this sort of scale and can be combined with other trailing foliages such as ivy and clematis, or the dark evergreen climber *rhoicissus* unravelled from the plant.

The medieval theme not only inspires an enchanting, jewel-like approach to colour, but allows a great deal of choice regarding containers. Huge urns made of stone, iron

TABLE ARRANGEMENT
(left)
*Designed to be viewed from
the front. the table
arrangement is a magnificent
cascade of blooms and foliage.
with royal purple anemones
adding visual depth. The
anemone has medieval
connections. as it is reputed to
have been first brought out of
the Holy Land during the
Crusades of the Middle Ages.*

HEADDRESS
(left)
*The flamboyant head pieces of
the medieval period, which
reached extraordinary heights
of elaborateness and
complexity, are the inspiration
for this lavish headdress.
Fittingly it is created on the
framework of a metal crown
and diamante decoration adds
a suitably majestic touch.*

or wood make a dramatic base for large imposing arrangements. Of course, it is not always practical to use very heavy props, and good-looking fibreglass or even plastic copies can be substituted. Such containers, when painted to imitate anything from marble to lichen-covered stone, have a very authentic medieval look. On a smaller scale, quirky little containers, each different, would be enchantingly original, although the materials should be 'medieval' ones, such as pewter, silver, wood, stone, crystal and glass; painted porcelain or patterned china would look inappropriate.

The medieval theme ranks as one of the most potent choices for wedding flowers. The quality of colour and bloom against dark glossy foliage, coupled with an imaginative choice of 'medieval' props and materials, can produce deeply satisfying and memorable results.

HEADDRESS

The bride's headdress is a grand affair, a flamboyant crown delicately entwined with ivy trails, and petals of the regal-looking gloriosa lily flickering like tiny flames around the deep purple anemones and blown orange roses. The flowers are wired individually and attached to a metal crown that is decorated with diamante, and the ivy is trailed around them (see page 138). The bride may prefer a simpler floral circlet of anemones, gloriosa and roses, or perhaps a wreath of gloriosa lilies and ivy around her head.

PALETTE OF
FLOWERS

'Tania' spray rose
Amaryllis
Anemone
Parrot tulip
Gloriosa lily

Birch twigs
Fatsia japonica leaves
Rosemary
Berried ivy
Trailing ivy
Mahonia
Cranberries

Gilded artichokes
Horse chestnuts
Walnuts
Pomegranates
Clementines

BRIDE'S BOUQUET
(left)
*The medieval theme lends
itself beautifully to a lavish use
of rich textures and materials
to accompany the flowers.
Fired by the sumptuous fabrics
of the period, the imagination
can be given free rein and a
magnificent array of damasks
and silks, velvets and satins, is
on offer for the choice of dress.*

WINTER

In the crisper air and starker
landscape of the winter months,
rare splashes of colour startle
and delight. With the pure lines of
bare branches, form and shape
are accentuated and pleasure taken
in subtle graduations which would
be lost against a more colourful
backdrop. The festivities of Christmas
and the birth of a new year add a
celebratory note to the season.

WINTER PROFUSION

The heady joy of a glorious display of elegant flowers usually associated with spring and summer is magnified by the use of heavily scented varieties. Despite the widespread idea that some flowers are difficult to get in winter time, there is, in fact, an extraordinary variety of lovely blooms available all year round, even in the coldest months. With the extension of the growing seasons of many plants and the importing of flowers from all over the world, there are now few limits to the possible combinations of colours, textures and shapes in any season.

The availability of out-of-season flowers is not a new phenomenon. From the seventeenth century and the advent of orangeries and hot houses, through every season the mansions of the wealthy have been resplendent with exotic species, heavy with the perfume of flowers imported from foreign climes, and showcases for rare blooms developed by the family gardeners.

Rich creams and greens are as much the colours of winter as are soft golds and browns, and snow whites. The foliage and flowers used here are equally beautiful when seen in daylight and when subtly altered by the candle- and lamplight in which they will often be seen in darker winter days. The exquisiteness of the shapes and the patterns they create are intricate parts of the arrangements.

To achieve a feeling of opulence, all the flower arrangements for this wedding are very large and dense. The individual blooms are rich and full, creating a feeling of festivity and extravagance. The use of such indulgent and wonderfully fragrant flowers as the beautiful trumpet-shaped 'Longiflorum' lily – and the confining of their use to the bride's bouquet and the large table arrangement – highlights the perfection of these blooms and the importance of the occasion. Notably absent from the bride's bouquet are the pink-tinged petals of the anemone which would have detracted from the purity of line and colour.

BRIDESMAID'S HOOP AND HEADDRESS
(left)
Rich shades of cream and an infinitely varied palette of greens are picked out by pale rays of wintry sunshine.

TABLE ARRANGEMENT
(left)
A loose profusion of twigs, lush foliage and elegant flowers is the perfect greeting for guests as they walk into an entrance hall.

GARLAND HEADDRESS
AND HOOP
(right)
The creamy shades of the
flowers are echoed in the
materials worn by the bride
and bridesmaid.

BRIDE'S BOUQUET
(right)
The appropriately named
shower bouquet creates a
charmingly loose effect.
Although roses and
'Longiflorum' lilies are the only
flowers featured, the use of
lush foliage makes the overall
result one of rich profusion.

GARLAND HEADDRESS

The most time-consuming arrangements are for the tiny bridesmaid. She wears a garland headdress, in which each flower or little grouping of flowers is wired and put together on a base wire (see page 138). White spray roses, white anemones and a touch of pink, the white helleborus known as the Christmas rose with its saucer-shaped petals and yellow anthers, and the light green guelder rose make a beautiful circlet. The ivy leaves are wired individually, as are the guelder rose leaves, and the jasmine leaves are left on the stem and entwined through the completed garland. Heavy headdresses like this one look enchanting, but not everyone suits them or has the right hairstyle. When making a garland headdress, it is important to take into account the size of the head.

HOOP

The hoop is made in a completely different way to the headdress (see page 138). To start with, a length of birch twigs is twisted and bound together with wire, then it is decorated with individually wired flowers and wrapped with trails of ivy. Another method is to make a garland, looser than for the headdress, and entwine it around the twig ring (see page 141).

An equally effective – and quicker – alternative to the bridesmaid's hoop would be a loose tied posy containing the same flowers and foliage. Or two bridesmaids could carry between them a lavish garland constructed on the same principle but on a much larger scale than the garland headdress (see Old-fashioned Roses, page 60).

BRIDE'S BOUQUET

The bride's shower bouquet (see page 136) is tied rather than wired and, consequently, has a loose feel to it and is less time-consuming to make. The profile of the flowers and foliage is important in creating the tumbling effect and to achieve a feeling of depth, materials need to be recessed deep into the arrangement (see page 136).

The spectacular 'Longiflorum' lily is the focal flower (see page 133) in the bouquet, accompanied only by white spray

HOOP
(left)
Contrasting and complementing textures are combined to splendid effect in the bridesmaid's hoop. Silken, perfectly formed white spray roses are framed by the matt green ivy leaves; the densely packed globes of the guelder rose are placed alongside the paper-thin blooms of the anemones.

TABLE ARRANGEMENT
(right)
A bright shaft of light picks out the strikingly sculptural 'Longiflorum' lilies.

PALETTE OF FLOWERS·

'Longiflorum' lily
Anemone
White spray rose
Christmas rose
(white hellebore)
Guelder rose
(Viburnum opulus)
Jasmine

Trailing ivy
Codiaeum leaves
Rhododendron leaves
Birch twigs
Fatsia japonica leaves

roses and three different types of foliage – the trailing ivy, the variegated leaves of the *codiaeum* plant, and the dark stiff leaves of the rhododendron. By starting with the main flowers the profile can be defined, with the transitional flowers (see page 133) and foliage worked around them. In this type of bouquet it is very effective to use only two or three types of flower, contrasting shapes, sizes and textures for maximum impact. This is particularly important when, as here, the palette of flowers and foliage is restricted to just white, cream and green.

TABLE ARRANGEMENTS
A charmingly unruly bundle of birch twigs is used as a background for the triangular arrangement designed for a corner table (see page 142). The container is filled with water and chicken wire, then the long-stemmed spiky guelder rose, regarded here as part of the foliage, is arranged after the birch twigs, before the elegant 'Longiflorum' lilies. White spray roses, jasmine and anemones are added next along with *Fatsia japonica* leaves and trailing ivy. This is a very simple arrangement, and one that is easy to create. The effect is loose and natural, because the birch twigs provide support and the shape of the flowers dictates the overall shape of the arrangement.

The church can be decorated with garlands or pew ends made of the foliage used in the bride's bouquet and the headdress. As these arrangements will be on a larger scale, alternative flowers that are less expensive but which have the same white and cream colours, perhaps with a touch of pale pink, may be chosen. White chrysanthemums or hydrangeas would be effective, as would clouds of gypsophila (baby's breath) or a few white rose buds finished with a satin bow. The total effect is what matters most in the church, as one walks into a cloud of glorious white blooms.

A CHRISTMAS WEDDING

COLOURS OF CHRISTMAS
(left)
Ruby red on ivory, with
Christmas tree greens – the
hues of this most festive
season set a majestic tone.

BRIDE'S HEADDRESS
(left)
The effect of a tiara is created
by building up roses and sprigs
of pine needles at the front of
the headdress; the use of ivy
leaves only at the back clearly
defines the shape.

Whether snow flakes are falling or a relentless sun is blazing, the Christmas season is traditionally associated with evergreens and deep reds, with pine trees and gold, swags and bells. A wedding at this most festive of times can be enriched with deep colour, fragrant with pine and glimmering with gold, and would be seen to full advantage in flickering candlelight.

Only one flower – the very dark red, almost black 'Baccarola' rose, a hybrid that looks like an old-fashioned bloom – is used in the bride's flowers, creating a sense of richness and drama. It is combined with variegated ivy leaves, sage green edged with silver, and spiky little sprigs of spruce. When gilded artichokes, pine and spruce cones are added the result is an exciting, almost medieval play of textures and colours.

For a Christmas wedding in the southern hemisphere at midsummer, when the sunlight can be harsh and a cooler effect is desired, roses and mistletoe would look appropriate, particularly in a bouquet incorporating gold bells.

BRIDE'S HEADDRESS

The ornate headpieces so beloved of medieval and Renaissance women are the inspiration for the bride's headdress, which is designed to sit on the head rather than encircle it. The 'Baccarola' roses and little sprigs of pine needles are confined to the front half of the headdress rather like a tiara, while variegated ivy leaves are used at the back. It is constructed in the same way as a garland headdress: before the material is taped on to a strong base wire, the ivy leaves are wired and stitched, each rose is wired and taped, and bunches of spruce are wired together (see page 134).

Once the base wire is decorated, a bend is made in the centre front. The headdress, which is slightly smaller than an ordinary garland headdress, is moulded into shape on the head then joined, so that it is pointed at the front and curves up at the sides then round and down at the back. Like the bouquet, the front of the headdress is entwined with gold bells knotted on to gold thread; other festive additions could include tiny gold cherubs or miniature gilded artichokes.

BRIDE'S BOUQUET

The intrinsic beauty of the roses inspires simplicity. In a round, hand-tied bouquet, they look like jewels, each perfect bloom outlined with ovate rose leaves and enhanced by the soft needles of the spruce foliage. Although it has an informal feel about it, the construction of the bouquet is carefully controlled. The stems of the roses and spruce are spiralled in the hand (see page 136), and three or four gilded artichokes, which have been wired and double-leg mounted (see page 134), are pushed deep into the arrangement. The artichokes are dried, coated with picture framer's gilding paint, then finished with a layer of thin, clear varnish; this technique creates a deep golden colour. The final touch is a gold thread on to which tiny gold metal bells are knotted at 5 cm (2 in) intervals; starting from the outside of the bouquet, the thread is knotted on to the stems of the roses, with the bells positioned in between, and swagged in a spiral which ends in the centre of the bouquet. Grosgrain ribbons in deep red and green are tied at the binding point and allowed to trail down. The whole effect is magnificent: as the bride moves, the bells jingle, the roses and foliage sway, and the artichokes and thread shimmer.

Although a long, trailing shower bouquet would work well (see page 136), it would be more difficult to incorporate the bells so effectively. With the round shape, it is possible to create depth and a sense of richness with very few materials.

BRIDE'S BOUQUET
Gilded artichokes pushed deep into the arrangement and tiny bells on golden thread heighten the rich, festive impact of the bouquet.

PALETTE OF FLOWERS

'Baccarola' rose
Amaryllis
'Longiflorum' lily

Ivy
Pine
Spruce
Gilded artichokes

SWAG

Dark red amaryllis and white 'Longiflorum' lilies are introduced into the very full swag which decorates the mantelpiece. They are a dramatic addition to the mass of foliage, made up of bunches of spruce and ivy trails, and gilded artichokes and pine and spruce cones, ornaments you expect to see on a Christmas tree, create visual interest and provide contrasting texture. Some antique velvet strawberries add an unexpected touch. The swag is made in three separate parts: two sides and a central piece. First of all, the swags for the sides are constructed from two trailing tied bunches (see page 141), the length being achieved with ivy and spruce branches. Bunches of spruce, 'Longiflorum' lilies, amaryllis and ivy are bound in and the side sections of the swag are fixed in position at each end of the mantelpiece. So that it hangs beautifully, the central piece, constructed like a garland (see page 141), is shaped like a crescent: thicker in the middle and tapering at the points where it is attached to the mantel. The flowers are bound in with the foliage, and ivy is then entwined around and allowed to trail down.

Paper ribbons – on one side finished with a gold cherub, on the other with gilded artichokes – catch the swag at the corners where the three pieces are joined.

Another, less expensive, approach would be to use only foliage with the cones, artichokes and other ornaments, perhaps adding in mistletoe, and finishing it with ribbons. Swags look wonderful slung from banister to banister; or three wreaths of the same materials hung over a fireplace can have an equally dramatic impact.

CAKE DECORATION

The mellow colours and rich textures are continued in the cake decoration. Little bells knotted on to gold thread are looped around the edge of the cake stands, secured by pins which are covered with glacé cherries and gooseberries and petals of the 'Baccarola' rose. More petals are scattered on top of the cake with gilded artichokes and gold chocolate dragées. Finally, roses and clementines are built up into a pyramid on top of the tiers. Ivy trails and golden bells are swagged around the edge of the table, in a simple but striking decoration in keeping with the festive tone.

SWAG
(far left)
*This gloriously full
arrangement is constructed in
three parts – on each side of
the mantelpiece a tied bunch is
attached to a central, crescent-
shaped garland.*

CAKE DECORATION
(left)
*Elements of the other
arrangements – 'Baccarola'
roses, gilded artichokes and
golden bells – are brought
together, along with glacé
fruits and gold dragées, to
decorate the tiers of the cake.*

VICTORIAN POSIES

BRIDE'S POSY
(left)
*Strikingly original materials
and a flawless construction
combine to perfection in this
posy of dried flowers and
shells.*

HORSESHOE
(left)
*The traditional symbol of good
luck carried by the bridesmaid
is a horseshoe of pink
rosebuds and globe
thistleheads, converging in the
centre on an exquisite spiral-
shaped shell.*

A Victorian drawing room would have been incomplete without some artfully arranged still life of shells and dried plants, stuffed animals and birds, butterflies or minerals, kept under a tall glass dome. One of the consuming passions of the age was the collecting and preservation of species, a pastime partly inspired by Charles Darwin's *The Origin of Species*.

These flowers are inspired by the beauty of the Victorian still life, using dried blooms and shells to recapture that earlier age's fascination with studying and controlling Nature. They have a vividness and immediacy lost in the dusty, faded originals. Today, dried flowers are not restricted to natural browns and creams, or dusty helichrysums and faded Chinese lanterns (*physalis*). Modern preservation methods use silica gel, which maintains the original colour of the bloom with a naturalistic result. Consequently, the colour range and the variety of dried flowers available are very wide. A wedding like this one, where all the flowers used are dried, is ideal for the winter when fresh blooms are expensive and the choice may be limited.

Here, the mellow-coloured compositions encompass a delicate palette of dusky pinks, sage greens, sun-bleached yellows and rosy reds, combined with the deep, rich blue of cornflowers and the hardness of small, prettily coloured shells. The little, spiky globe thistleheads are in sharp contrast to the smooth petals and compactness of the roses. The shiny satin ribbons glimmer beside the knotty-textured handmade lace that edges the bride's bouquet. The materials, although limited in quantity, are carefully chosen for their impact and distinctiveness.

BRIDE'S BOUQUET

Given the flowers, shells and the inspiration behind this wedding theme, it is appropriate that the bride's bouquet is a Victorian posy (see page 137). Each flower and globe thistlehead used in the posy is wired individually. The pretty white starfish shells are drilled and wired. The strawberry-coloured and the green shells are fitted with very strong florist's glue and tissue paper before a sturdy wire is pushed right in so that it hooks around the shell lip: for this kind of shell, this method gives more control than simply drilling and wiring. The preparation required for the posy is certainly time-consuming, as is the construction. However, the result is a beautifully finished posy that will not only look exquisite on the wedding day itself but which will last forever when preserved under an airtight dome of glass.

PALETTE OF FLOWERS

(dried)
Cornflower
Pink spray rose
Globe thistlehead
Nigella head

Birch twigs

Working from the central shell, the roses, cornflowers and thistles are alternated with the green and strawberry-coloured shells to make a regular design, and at the same time, the rows are gently contoured to make a pleasing dome shape. Finally, some beautiful antique lace is gathered around the edge. The lace needs to be fairly stiff, otherwise it will not stand up around the flowers.

HOOP

In the wonderful burnished gold of the winter sunlight, a tiny bridesmaid plays in the sand, collecting shells and little starfish to match those in her lovely ornamental hoop (see page 138). Birch twigs are twisted into a large hoop shape, which is decorated with nigella heads, dried cornflowers, pink spray roses and globe thistleheads, all of which are wired individually and then pushed into the hoop. The shells are glued on and wide pink ribbons add the finishing touch.

BRIDE'S POSY
(above)
An edging of delicate antique lace, matching the dresses worn by the bride and bridesmaid, puts the finishing touch to the posy.

BRIDESMAID'S HOOP
(right)
A simple hoop of birch twigs shows off the flowers and shells to great effect.

HORSESHOE

'The common People of this Country have a Tradition, that 'tis a lucky thing to find a Horseshoe', said the seventeenth-century Irish poet Roger Boyle. The tradition continues to this day and the bridesmaid carries a pretty floral horseshoe as a symbol of good luck. It is constructed on a base wire, with the rosebuds being built up from each end into double rows around the globe thistleheads; the spiral-shaped 'Terrebra Terrebra' shell is then glued on to the centre of the horseshoe to create a tiara-like effect.

VICTORIAN BATHING HUTS
The Victorian era is a rich source of inspiration for floral compositions.

HORSESHOE
(below)
The pastel shades of pink rosebuds complement beautifully the creamy sand-coloured hues of seashells.

VALENTINE WEDDING

It is a romantic bride indeed who chooses to wed on or around the feast of St Valentine, the 14th of February, for it is the one day of the year devoted to love and lovers. As long ago as the Middle Ages, writers and poets were evoking the saint in lines on love, and referring to the feast of St Valentine as the perfect time of year for the choosing of sweethearts – or the mating of birds. Perhaps it was simply the sight of doves cooing over each other that inspired the St Valentine tradition, which continues to this day with the sending of love tokens and anonymous messages to sighing lovers.

The flowers for a St Valentine's-Day wedding are rich in history and symbolism. Red roses are the universal symbol of true love, treasured for the longevity of their colour and their fragrant perfume, their peerless beauty and rich colour. Violets represent humility ('Where purple violets lurk, with all the lowly children of the shade' wrote the eighteenth-century poet James Thomson), grape hyacinths mean loveliness and constancy, white jasmine stands for amiability, and pansies symbolize remembrance.

Deep purples, blues and dark reds are colours that evoke passion rather than purity, as well as the intensity and turbulence of emotions associated with love. A softer, gentler approach would be to create a cherubic extravaganza of pinks and whites, adding clouds of gypsophila (which has the delightful, alternative name of baby's breath) to pink rosebuds, for example, and tying them with lace and ribbon to achieve a light and utterly romantic effect.

BRIDE'S BOUQUET
(left)
The intense colours of the bride's flowers – a combination of Valentine's Day red with sultry shades of purple – mirror the passions and depth of feeling associated with this most romantic day.

BUTTONHOLE
(above)
A cluster of flawless red spray roses is edged with individual rose leaves.

BRIDE'S BOUQUET

But this bride relishes the passion of the day, carrying a mass of red spray roses, grape hyacinths, violets and scarcely opened buds of laurustinus, arranged around some exquisite cream-edged deep purple pansies. Technically known as an Edwardian, or open, posy (see page 137), the bouquet differs from the Victorian posy in that it is not constructed in concentric circles and has a far looser and more natural appearance. But, because it is wired – the main flowers individually and the smaller, transitional ones (see page 133) in groups – the florist has a great deal of control over the materials. In any case, wiring is necessary for such short-stemmed, delicate flowers as the pansies and violas: the false stems that are added enable the flowers to be seen to effect in bouquets and headdresses without their delicate stems drying out.

Instead of the bouquet, the bride might carry a prayer book spray, a corsage-like arrangement (see page 139) that is constructed to sit on a prayer book or bible and which may be attached to a ribbon which is then used as a book marker. This has the advantage of being much smaller than the average bouquet, so the overall effect is much more low key, making it very suitable for a small-scale wedding in a church or registry office. Because only a limited number of blooms are used, the flowers in a prayer book spray need to be flawless and of sufficient distinction to stand alone.

COMB

In her hair, the bride wears a comb and veil, which is decorated very simply, using rosebuds, violets and jasmine which are wired and taped like a corsage (see page 139). A circlet or garland headdress made of the same combination of flowers used in the bride's bouquet would work equally well; indeed, it is particularly suitable for a St Valentine's Day wedding because the circle is a symbol of perfection, purity and eternal love.

TABLE DECORATIONS
(above)
Exquisite red spray roses define the heart shape of these glass dishes, with their edging of tiny violets. Interwoven jasmine trails provide a delightful backdrop.

COMB
(above left)
The intense shades of deep red and purple are relieved in this decoration by the fragile petals of white jasmine flowers.

TABLE DECORATIONS

The heart shape that is the signature of St Valentine's Day is repeated in the table decorations. A trio of heart-shaped glass dishes filled with roses and edged with violets, is interwined with white jasmine trails and pansies. One dish looks beautiful on a tiny drinks table surrounded by low candles, or a group can be arranged in a trail down the centre of a long buffet table or dining table. It is a very simple approach which achieves its effect by massing the flowers and using jasmine in its natural trails. And because the flowers are in water rather than florist's plastic foam, they will stay fresh for a long time.

An alternative, more formal table arrangement, perhaps in an entrance hall or on a side table, could use the flowers featured in the bride's posy and could echo its gentle dome shape. A low wickerware basket (see page 140) would be a delightful container which would not upstage the inherent drama of the flowers themselves.

PALETTE OF FLOWERS

Red spray rose
Violet
Pansy
Grape hyacinth (muscari)
Viola (heartsease)

Jasmine
Laurustinus *(Viburnum tinus)*
Syngonium foliage

FAVOUR BASKETS

For the favour baskets, wired flowers are stitched on to the basket rim with fine silver reel wire, which is easily pushed through the gaps in the weave; avoid using closely woven baskets (see page 142). The favour baskets are a charming addition to the wedding table, filled with chocolates and positioned by the place settings, instead of the traditional silk handkerchief of sugared almonds. They could be carried by small bridesmaids, although in this case it would probably be wiser to fill them with rose or other petals rather than with tempting chocolates.

BUTTONHOLES AND CORSAGES

At this most passionate of weddings, buttonholes and corsages add a striking finishing touch (see page 139). The strong colours and the shapes of the flowers used in these delicate arrangements provide a splendid opportunity to exploit the jewel-like qualities of the blooms. The buttonholes can be created from transient pansies and violas (heartsease) or from sturdier roses or little bunches of violets. Several blooms from one type of flower may be grouped together to create a totally different effect from using a single bloom, and it need not be any more bulky.

FAVOUR BASKETS
(left)
These heart-shaped baskets, edged with an array of wired flowers, could decorate a small drinks table or individual place settings.

BUTTONHOLES
(below left and centre)
AND CORSAGE
(below)
The dramatic colours of these flowers create a striking effect whether they are used as individual blooms or in delicate clusters.

PRACTICALITIES

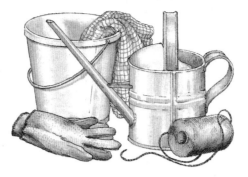

CHOOSING FLOWERS

Most people will probably start thinking about the wedding a long time in advance. However, while planning ahead is essential, you should also retain a certain amount of flexibility in deciding on your wedding flowers as seasonal availability and specific weather conditions will affect your choice.

Seasonal availability Flowers are actually at their best and at their cheapest when they are in season. Great advances have been made in forcing flowers in glasshouse conditions and using 'out-of-season' blooms can be an individual and striking approach. However, you should bear in mind that forced flowers are often less robust and are almost always much more expensive than those which are in season.

Weather conditions Most commercially produced flowers are grown under glass and are therefore protected, but extreme or irregular weather conditions can still affect those grown outside, damage foliage and delay or accelerate the blossoming of trees, for example. If the flowers you have chosen for the wedding are vulnerable, contingency plans should include alternative suppliers or alternative flowers.

Suppliers

Your choice is also going to be affected by the sources of flowers in your area. The main suppliers to consider are:

Florist's shops The more specialist shops will be able to obtain unusual blooms.

Flower stalls/markets Relatively cheaper, but may have a limited selection.

Specialist cultivators For example, rose growers, herbalists, antique flower growers, dried flower producers.

Private gardens Your own or a friend's garden may supply, for example, foliage, flowers which are not cultivated commercially or cottage garden flowers.

Wholesale flower markets These are cheap and will have a large selection for you to choose from, but they do not always sell to the general public.

TIMETABLE

Having chosen the flowers and the supplier, you need to turn your attention to the logistics of the day itself. It is not necessary to place a definite order until two weeks before the event and at that point the supplier should be able to tell you exactly what is available, how much it will cost and when you should collect the flowers – flowers in tight bud, for example, should be picked up a few days before the wedding.

When you start the actual arranging depends in part on the weather – flowers drop much more quickly in hot weather – and on access to the location. If possible, you may find it easier to make the unwired 'non-personal' arrangements the day before, either in situ or stored somewhere cool. The 'personal' items – the bouquet, headdresses and so on – can then be made on the morning of the wedding. Keep as many as possible of the unwired flowers standing in water and if it is very hot, spray the wired arrangements with water then keep them in the refrigerator until required.

CALCULATING QUANTITIES

Do not be daunted by the prospect of working out exactly what you need. Simply look at the requirements of each individual arrangement and multiply accordingly. Calculate the focal flowers, transitional flowers and foliage needed: a table arrangement, for example, may require 5 focal flowers, 15 transitional flowers and 1½ bunches of foliage. Multiply this by the total number of

table arrangements. Apply this approach to everything from buttonholes to swags.

ORGANIZING HELPERS

No doubt you will receive many offers of help and in deciding which offers to accept and which tasks to assign to whom, consider the following points:

Scale of the event

Restrictions on access If access to the building where the event is to be held is limited, you may require more people for a concentrated period of time.

Robustness of the flowers If the flowers are particularly delicate, they should be made as late as possible. Consider also whether any of the arrangements can be made in advance and kept in a cool place.

Make sure that everyone is thoroughly briefed on his or her role so the flowers are handled as little as possible.

CHECKLIST

In addition to the tools and materials which you need to create the arrangements themselves (see opposite page), the following equipment will also be useful:

1. Buckets
2. Watering can
3. Brooms and dustpans
4. Cloths
5. String or twine
6. Gardening gloves
7. Plastic rubbish bags
8. Stepladder

BRIEFING PROFESSIONALS

Should you decide to put the actual arranging into the hands of a professional, the first step is to find a suitable florist. Be prepared to put time and effort into this – it is important to find someone who can offer inspired, and practical, advice while still being prepared to interpret your own ideas. Take along photographs, fabrics and other materials which have provided your inspiration or which are a good starting point for a discussion of the effect you are aiming for.

CONDITIONING FLOWERS

The purpose of treating the stems of material is to encourage the intake of water so that the flowers will last longer. On *all* material you should:

1. Strip off all foliage which will be below the water line; otherwise, the leaves will rot.
2. Re-cut the stems. Make a slanting cut about 2.5 cm (1 in) up from the bottom of the stem and place the material immediately in cool water.

This is enough for most plants but some stems do benefit from extra attention:

Woody stems eg rhododendron, lilac
To encourage water intake, hammer the bottom 2.5 cm (1 in) of stem then scrape off another 2.5 cm (1 in) of bark above. Place the cut ends in boiling water for 30-60 seconds, then transfer to cool water.

Hollow stems eg delphinium, lupin, amaryllis
Turn the flower upside down and fill the stem with water. Plug the end with cotton wool and place a rubber band around the end of the stem to prevent it splitting.

Bleeding stems eg poppy, euphorbia
After cutting the stems, dip the cut ends in boiling water for 30 seconds to seal. Alternatively, singe the cut end with a match or candle flame until the end is blackened.

Roses Plunge the bottom 5 cm (2 in) of stem in boiling water for 2 minutes then place the flower up to the neck in cold water. Wilting roses can also be revived in this way.

Foliage Hammer or split the stem ends then immerse in water for several hours.

TOOLS & MATERIALS

Cellophane (1) is used to line containers that are not waterproof also, crumpled up, it serves as a plant support in its own right, particularly in see-through containers.

Chicken wire (2) is used to hold florist's plastic foam in position; also, crumpled up, it is used in containers as a plant support in its own right.

Florist's plastic foam (3) is soaked in water and used in containers to support flowers and foliage, which are pushed into it. If built up above the rim of the container, the water-

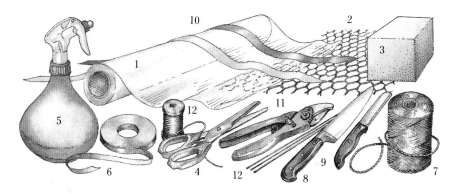

Flower arranging tools and materials.

retaining foam has the advantage of allowing the inserted materials to be angled over the sides. It should be held securely in position with florist's tape (a sticky variety) or chicken wire: chicken wire is more successful in large arrangements, because the foam has a tendency to crumble. The container should not be overfilled with foam: there should be enough room left so that water can be added whenever the foam is in danger of drying out.

Florist's scissors (4), which have a serrated edge, are essential for cutting stems; they can also cut wires and chicken wire.

A flower sprayer (5) is useful for refreshing flowers and foliage.

Florist's tape (6), also known as gutta-percha tape, is a rubber-coated tape used to cover wires and wired handles. A sticky variety is used to secure florist's plastic foam in position. The tape, which is available in white and green, should be stored in a cool place, otherwise it will perish.

Gardening twine (7), available in reels or balls, is used for binding in materials in tied posies and bouquets, and for securing binding points.

Knives (8/9) Two are required – a short one for scraping stems, and a long-bladed one for cutting wet florist's plastic foam.

Ribbon (10) is wound on to handles to cover wires on bouquets, posies, corsages and buttonholes; used decoratively in long trails and bows; and made into loops for garlands, swags and pomanders.

Secateurs (11) Used to cut woody stems.

Wires (12) Although there are almost a dozen gauges available for floristry work, only four are widely used:

0.90 mm (20 gauge) Used for wiring heavy flowers, such as heavy-headed lilies and foliage; available as stub wires.

0.71 mm (22 gauge) Used for wiring medium-strength flowers, such as roses and peonies; available as stub wires.

0.38 mm (28 gauge) Used for wiring more delicate flowers, such as violets; available as stub wires.

0.32 mm (30 gauge) Used for wiring very delicate flowers, such as lily-of-the-valley; available as stub wires and silver reel wire.

GLOSSARY OF TERMS

Focal material The main flowers or foliage in an arrangement to which the eye is drawn.

Profile The shape of an arrangement when viewed from the side.

Recess To place flowers deep in the arrangement so that the eye is drawn in and a feeling of visual depth is created.

Spiral To arrange the stems of material in the manner of a coil in order to build up the shape and profile of an arrangement.

Stitch To wire leaves (see page 134); also, to use reel wire to attach material.

Transitional material Flowers and foliage which link the focal elements of a design.

WIRING

Wiring flowers and leaves is necessary if the stems are delicate and if the materials have to be carefully controlled or contoured into a precise position – for instance, in some bouquets and posies, headdresses and corsages. Wiring can both strengthen the materials and make them more pliable.

Choose the right gauge of wire for the flower (see page 133). Do not bind wire over any foliage on the stem – make sure the twists of the wire go between leaves – and take care not to bruise soft stems.

Single-leg mount

1. Take the flower in your left hand (right, if left-handed) and rest the flowerhead on the top of the hand with the stem between the thumb and forefinger.
2. Place an appropriate wire horizontally behind the stem, one-third of the way up.
3. Close to make a hairpin with one short leg no longer than the natural stem and the other leg as long as required.
4. Hold the shorter leg down the side of the stem.
5. Twist the longer leg several times around the stem and short wire.
6. Straighten the long leg, which forms an extended stem.

Double-leg mount

1. Take the flower in your left hand (right, if left-handed) and rest the flowerhead on the top of the hand with the stem between your thumb and forefinger.
2. Place an appropriate wire horizontally behind the stem, about one-third of the way up, and with one-third of the wire on one side and two thirds on the other.
3. Close to make a hairpin with one leg approximately one-third longer than the other.
4. Hold the shorter leg down the side of the stem.
5. Twist the longer leg several times around the stem and shorter wire.
6. Straighten the legs, which should now be roughly equal in length, to form a double-leg mount.

Hollow stemmed material

Push a piece of stub wire with a smaller diameter gauge up inside the stem into the base of the flower.

Pipping

Delicate blooms, such as delphinium and foxglove flowers, which have been picked from the main flowerhead are very delicate and need to be supported.

1. Take an appropriate wire and make an 'eye' at one end.
2. Push the wire down through the flowerhead so the 'eye' lodges in its neck.
3. Then double-leg mount the false stem and tape.

Stitching leaves

1. Hold a leaf upside down in your left hand (right, if left handed).
2. Using an appropriate gauge silver stub wire, make a small horizontal stitch in the central vein, two-thirds of the way up the leaf. The stitch should not be noticeable from the front.
3. Bend the wire down to form a hairpin.
4. Twist one of the legs around the other leg and the stem to form either a single-leg or double-leg mount.

Extending the length of the stem

Flowers with delicate stems, such as violas and pansies, may need extra support.

1. Leave on 1.5 cm (½ in) of natural stem.
2. Push a stub wire horizontally through the base of the flower.
3. Bend the lengths of wire down and twist them around the stem several times.
4. Then single-leg mount the wired flower and tape if required.

SINGLE-LEG MOUNT   DOUBLE-LEG MOUNT   PIPPING   STITCHING LEAVES   EXTENDING STEMS

TAPING

1. Hold the flower in your right hand (left, if left-handed) between your thumb and forefinger, with florist's tape between the thumb and forefinger of the other hand.
2. Working from the top of the wire mount, hold the tape stretched taut against the flower at a 45° angle.
3. Twist the flower carefully upwards, at the same time stretching the tape a little with your other hand, so that the tape covers the wire right down to the base of the mount.
4. Twist the tape on to itself to seal.

FINISHING A HANDLE

1. Trim the wire handle to 1.5 cm (½ in) wider than the diagonal across the palm of the hand.
2. Cover the tip of the handle by placing the end of the ribbon behind it, then bringing it round and approximately halfway up the front.
3. Twist the ribbon around the handle to the bottom.
4. Then double back up the handle, this time twisting the *handle* and not the ribbon. Keep the ribbon taut so that the handle is completely covered.
5. Secure the ribbon at the top with a slip knot and make a bow to finish the bouquet.

MAKING A BOW

1. Take a length of ribbon and make a loop, leaving a generous amount over.
2. Hold the ribbon at the cross-over point, and make another loop to create a figure-of-eight.
3. Make two more loops in the same way, centering them on the same point.
4. Cut the loose ends of the ribbon at an angle.
5. At the back of the bow, gather the ribbon at the cross-over point to bring the centre together.
6. Wind reel wire or another piece of ribbon several times around the gathered centre of the ribbon to secure the bow. Knot and cut the wire or ribbon at the back.

DRYING FLOWERS
Air drying

This is the most widely used – and easiest – method of drying flowers. It is equally successful for individual flowers and foliage and for made-up arrangements. Simply hang the flowers upside down in a warm room, away from direct sunlight, which will fade the colours. Airing cupboards are usually too dry; choose a room with good air circulation. The drying process takes two to three weeks.

Silica gel

Flowers that are preserved in silica gel crystals retain their colours better than if air dried. The drying method is simple: the material to be dried is buried in a container of silica gel crystals. Cover the base of the container with crystals, place the plant material on top and then carefully cover it with more silica gel so that all the flower-heads and leaves are completely immersed – if necessary, use a small spoon to distribute the crystals between the flowers so no air gaps are left. Seal the container. Check the arrangement after two days, and remove as soon as it has dried. If indicator crystals have been used, they will turn pink when the material has dried.

Crystals can be reused: dry out by placing on a tray in a warm oven.

Glycerine

This is best used for foliage only, but has the disadvantage of changing the colours considerably. Stand the stems of the plant material in a container filled with a solution of 40 per cent glycerine and 60 per cent almost-boiling water; keep in a cool, dark place. Check after about a week: the material has dried out when the colour has changed substantially.

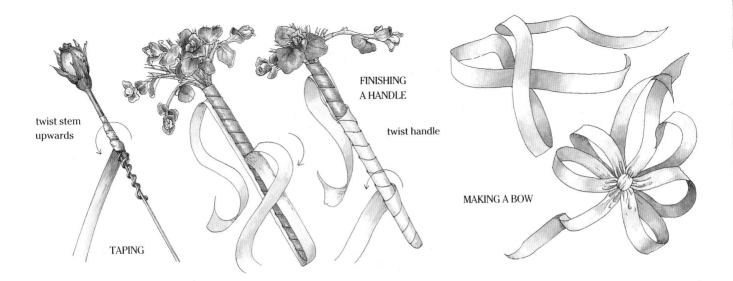

twist stem upwards

TAPING

FINISHING A HANDLE

twist handle

MAKING A BOW

SPIRALLED HAND-TIED POSY
(eg Harvest Thanksgiving)

1. Select a large flower or group of flowers for the centre.

2. Lay another flower at an angle to one side of the central flower, holding them at the binding point. Two-thirds of the arrangement should be above the binding point and one-third, taken up by the stems, should be below. (The distance of the binding point from the head determines the width of the final bouquet.)

3. Keep adding the flowers and angling them, rotating the posy in your hand and gradually building up the required shape and profile of the arrangement. (It may help to do this in front of a mirror so that you can see the shape.)

4. As the size of the bouquet increases, the stems make a spiral shape. Place the flowers or foliage with strong stems at the edge to protect those with more delicate stems.

5. Check the finished posy; if necessary, push some flowers deep into the posy to create visual depth.

6. Tie the binding point with gardening twine. Trim stems to required length (the stems below the binding point should be slightly longer than the diagonal across the palm of the hand).

7. Cover the twine with a bow.

SPIRALLED HAND-TIED POSY

binding point

Angle stems and rotate the posy
to form a spiral shape.

SPIRALLED TIED SHOWER BOUQUET
(eg Winter Profusion)

1. Make the triangular outline with foliage, using shorter lengths on the outer edges and graduating to a longer point in the centre. (It may help to do this in front of a mirror so that you can see the shape.) The binding point should be directly behind the focal point, which should be one-third of the way down the bouquet.

2. Start adding the flowers and angling them, defining the final shape of the bouquet with transitional materials and positioning the focal flowers as you work.

3. As the size of the bouquet increases, the stems make a spiral shape.

4. Check the finished bouquet; if necessary, recess some flowers for visual depth.

5. Tie the binding point with gardening twine. Trim stems to required length (the stems below the binding point should be slightly longer than the diagonal across the palm of the hand).

6. Cover the twine with a bow.

WIRED SHOWER BOUQUET
(eg Perfume in Springtime)

1. Select the flowers and foliage to be used, grading according to the size of heads or leaves. Lay them on a table to get the shape of the bouquet. Cut the stems to length, according to final position in bouquet (the smallest blooms are used at the end of the bouquet and therefore have the longest stems; the largest flowers are used as the focal point and so have the shorter stems).

2. Wire and tape every stem. Prepare foliage either by stitching and mounting leaves individually, or mounting trails or branches.

3. Using silver reel wire, bind in the flowers so that the binding point is behind the focal flower or flowers (about one-third of the way down the finished bouquet).

4. Build up the arrangement carefully, varying the angles at which the flowers and

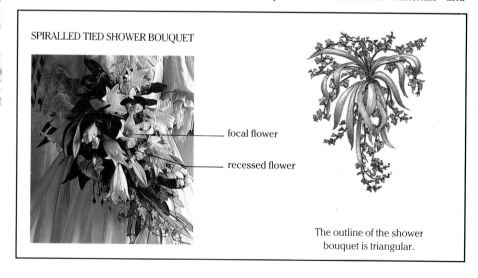

SPIRALLED TIED SHOWER BOUQUET

focal flower

recessed flower

The outline of the shower
bouquet is triangular.

EDWARDIAN POSY

focal flower

Bend seven sets of wired
flowers outwards at a 90° angle
to form a circle.

foliage are wired into the binding point to create an interesting profile, and recessing some blooms. Keep the binding point constant as each flower or leaf is added; if the material which has already been wired in moves, it can be easily adjusted.

For a crescent-shaped bouquet, angle the material above the focal flower (the top third of the bouquet) so that it curves back over the wrist.

5. Once the bouquet is finished, continue to wind the reel wire down the handle to secure. Trim the handle of the bouquet (it should be a little wider than the diagonal made by the palm of the hand).

6. Tape and ribbon the handle, then finish with a bow if required.

VICTORIAN POSY
(eg Victorian Posies)

1. Wire and tape every stem (or wire delicate or very small flowers such as violas and lilies-of-the-valley into groups and tape). Stitch, mount and tape foliage.

2. Select a large flower or group of flowers for the centre.

3. Lay another flower at an angle to one side of the central flower and bind in with reel wire, holding at the binding point. (The distance of the binding point from the head determines the width of the final bouquet.)

4. Keep binding in materials to create a regular concentric pattern: make each circle of the same flower or group of flowers, or of two different flowers alternated. As you add them, angle the materials, rotating the posy in your hand, and gradually building up the required shape and domed profile.

5. To complete the posy, edge with stiff lace. Stitch silver wire in gathering stitch along the inner edge of the lace; place lace around the binding point and pull wire in to gather. Hold the lace in position with a layer of stitched and mounted leaves which are bound in with silver reel wire.

6. Tape and ribbon the handle.

EDWARDIAN POSY
(eg Valentine Wedding)

1. Leave the flowers and foliage on their natural stems. Wire and mount them, to extend the stems, and then tape the stems individually.

2. Tape together seven sets of two flowers each, positioning a smaller flower or bud at the top.

3. Wire the seven sets of flowers together with silver reel wire, bending them out to form a circle, the spokes of which are evenly spaced; the extended wire mounts, which should be at a 90° angle to the flowers, then form the handle.

4. Position seven pieces of foliage between the flower spokes and bind in.

5. Insert the focal flower or flowers in the centre of the circle; its wired and taped stem(s) should be as long as those of the two-flower sets.

6. Add seven smaller flowers around the focal flower. Position them in line with the flower spokes and slightly lower than the focal flower.

5. Fill in the spaces with flowers and foliage, gradually building up the required profile.

6. Check the finished posy; if necessary, push some flowers deep into the posy to create visual depth.

7. Tape and ribbon the handle.

VICTORIAN POSY

circles of material

As each circle is added to the
posy, angle the materials to
create a dome shape.

GARLAND HEADDRESS

1. Cut the flowers, leaving 1.5 cm (½ in) of natural stem, then wire individually or in little bunches and tape. Stitch and mount individual leaves if required, then tape.
2. Decide on the sequence in which the flowers and foliage are to be used; this is important to ensure that the headdress looks even.
3. Using silver reel wire, bind one flower or bunch on to another. Space them according to thickness required, covering each stem or bunch of stems with the flowers of the next. Continue until the bound material is long enough to fit the head (the average size of a child's head usually ranges from 47.5-52.5 cm (19-21 in), an adult's from 50-55 cm (20-22 in).)
4. Join by binding the reel wire through the materials at the beginning of the garland.
5. The material should be distributed evenly on the headdress. If the garland needs extra fullness, push in more wired and taped flowers and foliage.
6. If required, wind ivy or other trailing material around the flowers and foliage.

GARLAND HEADDRESS ON A MAIN STAY WIRE

1. Prepare the flowers as above.
2. To make a main stay wire, tape together four 0.71 mm (gauge 22) wires, staggering each wire, and adding in new ones as

TWIG HOOP

circle of birch twigs

Bend birch twigs round and
secure to form a circle.

required to obtain the desired length. Make the stay wire 4 cm (1½ in) longer than the head circumference. (The average size of a child's head usually ranges from 47.5-52.5 cm (19-21 in), and an adult's from 50-55 cm (20-22 in).)
3. Decide on the sequence in which the flowers and foliage are to be used; this is important to ensure that the headdress looks even.
4. Tape the flowers on to the main stay wire to cover it, leaving the extra 4 cm (1½ in) free on one end; shape the wire into a circle as you work.
5. When the headdress is the desired size, overlap the undecorated wire at the back,

and tape through the flowers to secure.
6. If a tiara effect is required, tape more flowers on to the front half of the headdress.
7. If ivy or other trailing plant material is to be used, wind it through the headdress.

TWIG HOOP

1. Make a large circle out of birch twigs twisted together. Secure by binding the loose twig ends together with wire.
2. Wire flowers individually or in bunches. Stitch and mount leaves or wire in bunches.
3. Push the flowers and foliage into the hoop, weaving their wires between twigs to secure. Cover the hoop evenly.
4. If using, glue on shells, wrap ivy or other trailing plant material around the materials on the hoop.

METAL HOOP

1. Wire flowers individually or in bunches. Stitch and mount leaves or wire in bunches.
2. Tape flowers, foliage and bunches on to the metal hoop, facing them towards the front of the hoop and positioning each over the stems of the one before.

   Alternatively, wire individual, strong-stemmed unwired flowers, such as marguerites, left with long stems measuring about 20 cm (8 in), directly on to the hoop, positioning them in a cartwheel pattern.
3. If required, decorate the hoop with ribbons tied in bows.

GARLAND HEADDRESS

GARLAND HEADDRESS
ON A MAIN STAY WIRE
Tape on material so that each bunch
covers the stems of the last.

POMANDER

1. For a 20 cm (8 in) diameter pomander, take a small piece of wet florist's plastic foam and round the corners. Cover with a piece of chicken wire to make a globe the size of a tennis ball.
2. Make a loop with a piece of ribbon. Stitch its two ends together with reel wire, then twist this around the chicken wire.
3. Hang the ball up to decorate it.
4. Push foliage into the foam, distributing it evenly to cover the pomander completely.
5. Push in flowers and other decoration, individually wired if necessary, distributing them evenly.

POMANDER

Push foliage into the foam, distributing it evenly.

BUTTONHOLES

1. Wire, mount and tape flowers. The stems of small, delicate flowers can be wired together in groups.
2. Prepare the foliage by stitching the leaves individually. Cover the wires with tape.
3. Position the flowers or groups of flowers so that the binding point is behind the focal flower or group, binding each addition in with silver reel wire.
4. Place the leaves behind the flowers – graded according to size, with the largest leaf at the top working round to the two smallest at the bottom.
5. Cut the wires to the required length and cover with tape.
6. Attach a pin for securing the buttonhole.

CORSAGE

1. Prepare flowers by wiring and mounting on support wires, as necessary (see Wiring, page 134); cover with tape.

Flowers with very delicate stems such as pansies and violets should be treated in groups: first they are double-leg mounted on support wires, then double-leg mounted again and taped.
2. Prepare the foliage by stitching the leaves individually. Cover the wires with tape.
3. Position the flowers so that the binding point is behind the focal flower or group (in the centre if the corsage is round; about one-third of the way down if it is shaped) and so that the corsage curves a little if

required; bind each addition with fine silver reel wire.
4. If the corsage is round, position leaves as for buttonhole.

For a shaped corsage, position the leaves behind the flowers – graded according to size, with the largest leaves around the focal flower, working round to the two smallest at the bottom.

If the corsage is intended to curve over the shoulder (see Art Nouveau), bend back the top flowers.
5. Cut the wires to the required length and cover wire with tape.
6. Attach a pin so that the corsage can be secured in the required position.

BUTTONHOLE

focal flower

CORSAGE

focal flower

The binding point should be behind the focal flower.

BASKET

1. Line the basket with plastic and fill with wet florist's plastic foam to a height just above the rim. Push a wire from one side to the other through the centre of the foam and wind ends around the handle; alternatively, secure the foam with florist's sticky tape, which is wound round the base of one side of the handle, pulled taut over the foam and secured to the handle on the other side.

2. Create an outline using the foliage. The scale and shape of the arrangement depend on the size of the basket and the variety and shape of the materials. The final result may be round or oval, domed or trailing.

If the basket is to be carried, leave enough room around the handle for it to be held comfortably: about 2.5 cm (1 in) for a child, 4-5 cm (1½-2 in) for an adult.

3. Position the largest focal flowers in the centre of the arrangement, grading down to the smaller ones towards the edges.

4. Continue by positioning transitional flowers evenly throughout, reinforcing the outline shape. For more formal arrangements, the transitional flowers can be positioned in

TIED BOUQUET IN A BASKET

— spiralled stems

— binding point

Before binding arrange the material loosely in the basket to check the balance.

regular patterns – for example, the cream sweet peas used in Perfume in Springtime (see page 16) are placed along one diagonal, and the white sweet peas along an opposing one. To create visual depth, vary the height of some of the flowers occasionally without altering the overall shape of the arrangement.

5. If using a light frothy flower, such as gypsophila or dill, add this last.

6. If required, cover the handle with ribbon.

RIBBONING A HANDLE

1. Make two small bows (see page 135).

2. Wire a long piece of ribbon to one of the bows.

3. Wire this bow to the base of the handle at one side, then wind the attached ribbon over the handle to cover completely.

4. Secure on the other side by wiring on the other bow.

TIED BOUQUET IN BASKET

1. Arrange the flowers and foliage you plan to use in the basket loosely, to check balance. Because the bouquet is weighty, it must be carefully balanced, for visual as well as practical reasons. This is why long stems are left on the materials. Generally, two-thirds of the whole arrangement is in the basket, and half of this is taken up by the stems.

2. Make the bouquet by spiralling the stems in the hand. The bouquet should have a fairly flat back, and be gently profiled.

Alternatively, construct the bouquet on a framework of foliage and then push in the flowers, which are angled to give a profile to the bouquet.

4. Tie the bouquet with gardening twine, then wire it into the basket at the binding point: wind the wire around the binding point, then push the two ends of wire through gaps in the basket and secure them.

5. If required, disguise the binding point with a bow.

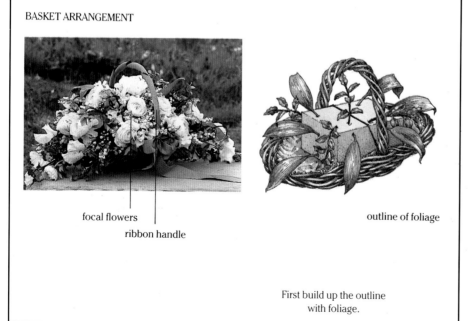

BASKET ARRANGEMENT

focal flowers

ribbon handle

outline of foliage

First build up the outline with foliage.

MANTELPIECE SWAG GARLAND

1. If the swag is made up of several loops, construct each section separately. For each section, wire the flowers individually or in bunches, then tape.

2. Using gardening twine, bind one flower or bunch on to another or on to a rope. Space them according to thickness required, covering each stem or bunch of stems with the flowers of the next.

Continue adding materials, building up the thickness of the swag towards the centre and keeping the ends thinner, to make a crescent shape.

3. The materials should be distributed evenly. If the swag needs extra fullness, push in more flowers and foliage.

4. If using ivy or other trailing plants, wind around the bound flowers and foliage to give a natural, loose flowing effect.

5. If it is made in sections, attach the swag to the mantelpiece or table by hooking over nails or pins.

6. Cover joins with big ribbon bows if required, or more flowers.

DOOR SWAG

1. Choose a long piece of foliage which curves gracefully, and use that as a base for the arrangement.

2. Insert more foliage to make a triangular-shaped outline, as for a tied shower bouquet (see page 134), binding in with gardening twine and building up the composition above the binding point.

The binding point may be at the side rather than at the centre of the swag; in any case, it should be positioned about one-third of the way down the finished swag. Below the binding point, add foliage following the natural shape of the base material. Use materials of varying lengths in order to create an interesting profile on the front of the swag; the back should be flat so that it can be attached to the door.

3. Push flowers into the swag, concentrating them near the binding point and reducing their frequency further away from this point.

4. Finish by making a wire loop over the binding point. Hang on a nail or a hook on the door.

DOOR SWAG — binding point — flat back — profile

The profile of a door swag is very important.

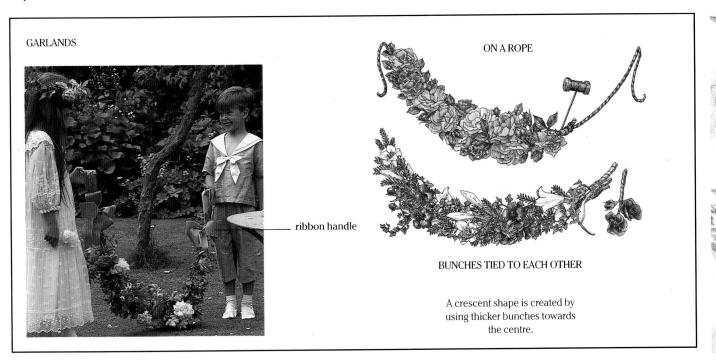

GARLANDS

ribbon handle

ON A ROPE

BUNCHES TIED TO EACH OTHER

A crescent shape is created by using thicker bunches towards the centre.

TABLE ARRANGEMENT

1. If it is a large arrangement, create it in situ because it will be difficult to move once it is finished. Protect the table surface or tablecloth with a plastic sheet while the arrangement is being done.

2. First, prepare the container.

If the container is not watertight, or if water would damage it, it should be lined with plastic or a sheet of cellophane. A block of florist's plastic foam is then placed on top and the flowers are arranged in that.

Alternatively, if the container is large, a smaller bowl or bucket can be placed inside it and the flowers then arranged in the smaller container, supported by either chicken wire or foam if necessary.

However the container is lined, next build up blocks of florist's plastic foam above the lip of the container and mould chicken wire over the foam to secure it and keep it from crumbling. (The higher the foam, the more the flowers and foliage can be angled to create a tumbling effect.) Fill with water.

A watertight container should be filled with water and crumpled-up chicken wire. If the container is glass, scrunched-up cellophane can be used to support the flowers.

3. Cut the stems of the materials to length. The tallest materials should be about twice the height of the container to be visually balanced.

4. Create the outline of the arrangement with foliage and transitional material, inserting the materials that define the arrangement's height, width and overall shape and keeping in mind the way the materials grow naturally. Outer stems can be angled downwards so they trail loosely over the rim.

Take into account where the arrangement is to be placed. If it is to be seen from all sides, work all the way round, so there is no 'front' and 'back'.

5. Add in the focal flowers.

PEW END

1. Make the outline with foliage, keeping the back flat. The binding point should be directly behind the focal point, which should be one-third of the way down the arrangement.

2. Add more materials and angle them, defining the final shape of the decoration with transitional materials, using their natural shapes to advantage with long curved stems trailing down.

3. Tie the binding point with gardening twine. Cover with ribbon, then tie the ribbon over the back of the pew end to secure.

4. When the arrangement is in place, push additional flowers or ornaments, which have been wired if necessary, deep into the binding point.

An alternative for a pew end is to make the arrangement in a special frame, available from florist's suppliers. The frame is filled with wet plastic foam and the flowers and foliage are arranged in that.

TABLE ARRANGEMENTS

dome shape

focal flowers

outline of foliage

Build up the outline of the arrangement with foliage.

outline of foliage

Create a full outline with foliage.

INDEX

ACKNOWLEDGMENTS

Conran Octopus would like to thank the following for their help
with locations and props:

Basia Zarzycka
E3, Chenil Galleries
181 King's Road
London SW3 5UB

Best of British Craft Shop
27 Shorts Gardens
London WC2

Beverly Summers
36 Shorts Gardens
London WC2

Catherine Buckley
302 Westbourne Grove
London W11 2PS

Charles H Fox Ltd
22 Tavistock Street
London WC2

Cushions and Covers
571 King's Road
London SW6

Decorative Art
C2, Chenil Galleries
181 King's Road
London SW3 5UB

Dining Room Shop
62/64 White Hart Lane
London SW13

Gallery of Antique
    Costume and Textiles
2 Church Street
London NW8

Hackett Clothiers
117 Harwood Road
London SW6

The Hop Shop
Castle Farm
Eynsford
Kent

Jans Ou Daatje (Luggage)
Chenil Galleries
181 King's Road
London SW3 5UB

Lyn Lundie (Dresses)
47 The Market
Covent Garden
London WC2

Monkey Island Hotel
Bray on Thames
Berkshire

Perfect Glass
5 Park Walk
London SW10

Persiflage
Chenil Galleries
181 King's Road
London SW3 5UB

Snapdragon Ltd
167-169 Dawes Road
London SW6

Stitches and Daughters
Tranquil Vale
London SE3

Tobias and the Angel
68 White Hart Lane
London SW13

Tom Gilbey's Waistcoat Gallery
2 Burlington Place
London W1

Special thanks to Sara Bertioli, 37 High Street, Sevenoaks, Kent, for
the loan of wedding gowns, and to all the following people for their
very generous help with photography:

Abigail Ahern, Fleur Barber, Nadine Bazar, Eedie Berry, Karley &
Janet Bedford, Zoe Brown, Rodney Compton, Emmie Cooper, Mrs S
Crang, Camilla & Sue Dann, Mr & Mrs George Evans, Matt Hall, Julia
& Ray Head, Rory Higham, Kathleen Hudson, Ruth Johnson, Mr &
Mrs P Keats, Nicky Lewis, Anna Moulding, Mr & Mrs Peregrine
Palmer of Dorney Court, Dorney, Berkshire, Rachel Perry, Jane &
Sophie Rees, Cherry Scott, Jeffrey Spencer, Matthew Targett, Kai &
Kaja Tveite-Weller, Alex Walter, Jessica Walton, Ruth White.

The author would also like to thank Fleur Barber, Willie, and, at
New Covent Garden Market, London SW8, Dennis, Lee and David of
John Austin & Co. and David Bacon of A & F Bacon.

The jacket design and pages 132-142 incorporate a reproduction of
hand-made paper from the Richard de Bas paper mill at Ambert,
France.